William Wordsworth

THE RUINED COTTAGE
The Brothers
Michael

William Wordsworth

THE RUINED COTTAGE
The Brothers
Michael

Edited with a critical introduction and notes by
Jonathan Wordsworth

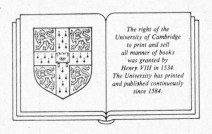

The right of the
University of Cambridge
to print and sell
all manner of books
was granted by
Henry VIII in 1534.
The University has printed
and published continuously
since 1584.

Cambridge University Press

Cambridge
London   New York   New Rochelle
Melbourne   Sydney

Contents

Note on texts

The texts in this volume are those prepared for the forthcoming Cambridge *Wordsworth*, and I am grateful to the Trustees of Dove Cottage for permission to print from manuscripts at the Wordsworth Library, Grasmere. Original spelling has been retained; ampersands have been eliminated; and in words that are no longer likely to be mispronounced, apostrophe 'd' has been replaced by the normal 'ed'. Initial capital letters, which in the manuscripts (and in general among Wordsworth's contemporaries) are frequent but inconsistent, have been retained only for 'God' and 'Nature'.

Published by the Press Syndicate of the University of Cambridge
The Pitt Building, Trumpington Street, Cambridge CB2 1RP
32 East 57th Street, New York, NY 10022, USA
10 Stamford Road, Oakleigh, Melbourne 3166, Australia

© Jonathan Wordsworth 1985

First published 1985

Printed in Great Britain at the University Press, Cambridge

Library of Congress catalogue card number: 84 – 12126

British Library Cataloguing in Publication Data
Wordsworth, William, *1770–1850*
The Ruined Cottage, The Brothers, and Michael
I. Title   II. Wordsworth, Jonathan
821'.7   PR5853
ISBN 0 521 26525 8 hard covers
ISBN 0 521 31936 6 paperback

WD

Introduction

Writing to a friend in 1818, Keats claimed that Wordsworth was a greater poet even than Milton, because he 'thinks into the human heart'.[1] One of the poems that he must certainly have had in mind is *The Ruined Cottage*, published in 1814 as Book I of *The Excursion*, but first written in 1797–8 as an independent work. With *The Brothers* and *Michael*, both of 1800, *The Ruined Cottage* forms a closely knit group of tragic poems that are central to Wordsworth's poetry of the human heart. As a result of being incorporated in a longer work, rather than published separately, *The Ruined Cottage* has been comparatively little known.[2] In 1969, however, it was printed from a manuscript of 1799 preserved at the Wordsworth Library in Grasmere, and it is now firmly established as a great poem in its own right. It is presented below for the first time in a fully annotated and readily available edition.[3] *The Brothers* and *Michael* were published by Wordsworth himself within months of their composition; they are presented here in the text of *Lyrical Ballads* 1800, but with annotation derived from the manuscripts. Punctuation in all three texts is editorial.

The three poems in this volume have it in common that they are about love, and about the feelings of the survivor in a broken relationship. Margaret loses her husband, Leonard his brother, Michael his only son. Wordsworth draws our attention to their suffering not because he is morbidly interested in pain, but because, like Shakespeare, he sees it as capable of bringing out the deepest and noblest human emotions. 'Action', he writes in his play, *The Borderers* (1796–7),

> is transitory – a step, a blow,
> The motion of a muscle this way or that . . .

[1] Keats to John Hamilton Reynolds, 3 May 1818.
[2] For a brief outline of the different changes that *The Ruined Cottage* went through before becoming part of *The Excursion*, see Notes, below.
[3] For the first publication of *The Ruined Cottage* as a separate work, see Jonathan Wordsworth, *The Music of Humanity* (London and New York, 1969). More recently the poem has been edited by James A. Butler, with full textual apparatus and photographs of the surviving manuscripts, as a volume in the Cornell Wordsworth Series (Ithaca, N.Y., 1979) – 'Butler' in future references.

Suffering, by contrast,
                    is permanent, obscure and dark,
          And has the nature of infinity.
                    (*Borderers*, III. v. 60–5)

They are strange words to choose, but they tell us a lot about the poet
and his beliefs. Actions, incidents, exciting events, have no place in
his work – they themselves are too soon over, and so is the pleasure
they stir in the reader. Suffering is different: it does not just happen,
it goes on. It is 'obscure and dark' because it cannot be defined, or
comprehended; and it 'has the nature of infinity' because it possesses
the quality that Wordsworth valued above all, of seeming no longer to
be bounded by the limits of ordinary existence.

   In another sense, of course, ordinariness is what Wordsworth
claimed to be writing about. He told Henry Crabb Robinson in 1837
that he wanted to be remembered only

for the way in which his poems exhibit man in his essentially human
character and relations – as child, parent, husband – the qualities which
are common to all men, as opposed to those which distinguish one man
from another.[1]

But there are no lowest common denominators in Wordsworth's
poetry. Hazlitt described him as having 'a levelling muse', yet this is
true only in social terms. The Preface to *Lyrical Ballads* makes it clear
that Wordsworth chooses ordinary country people as a way of making
claims that are not ordinary at all:

Low and rustic life was generally chosen because in that situation the
essential passions of the heart find a better soil . . . are less under restraint,
and speak a plainer and more emphatic language.

The 'qualities that all men have in common' are not those which are
usually seen in our behaviour 'as child, parent, husband'. They are
'the *essential* passions of the heart', the deep underlying emotions
which we are normally least able to show.

   To Wordsworth it seemed that the task of the poet was to record
these feelings – and to do so in such a way as to make others experi-
ence, through the poetry, emotions that were equally 'sane, pure, and
permanent'.[2] Read with this in mind, the Preface to *Lyrical Ballads* may

---

[1] *Henry Crabb Robinson on Books and Their Writers*, ed. E.J. Morley (3 vols., London,
1938), II, 535.

[2] As well as reflecting faithfully the feelings of human nature, Wordsworth
commented to John Wilson in a letter of 7 June 1802, a great poet 'ought to a
certain degree to rectify men's feelings . . . to render their feelings more sane,
pure, and permanent, in short, more consonant to Nature – that is, to eternal
Nature, and the great moving spirit of things', *Letters of William and Dorothy
Wordsworth: The Early Years* ('*EY*' in future references), revised by Chester L.
Shaver, Oxford, 1967, p. 355.

be seen as the poet's quest for a permanent language in which to evoke what appeared to him essential, and therefore unchanging, in human emotion.[1] Perhaps few people would now agree that 'Poetry is the first and last of all knowledge . . . as immortal as the heart of man' (Preface to *Lyrical Ballads*); but for those who have any degree of sympathy for what Wordsworth was trying to say, *The Ruined Cottage*, *The Brothers* and *Michael* will be very important poems. Each shows him truly thinking into the heart, exploring with a profound tragic intuition what is 'immortal', infinite, in the suffering and hope of an individual human being.

It is important to notice that for the reader of these poems, optimism is made impossible. We are asked to share the 'torturing hope' of the central characters, but we have before us from the first the evidence that hope was pointless. In the case of *The Ruined Cottage*, Wordsworth seems not only to have begun with the tragic outcome of his story in mind, but actually to have started writing at the end. Among the first sequences to be composed is his conclusion, describing the final years and death of the heroine:

> '[On this old bench
> For hours she sate, and evermore] her eye
> Was busy in the distance, shaping things
> That made her heart beat quick. Seest thou that path? –
> The green-sward now has broken its grey line –
> There to and fro she paced through many a day
> Of the warm summer, from a belt of flax
> That girt her waist, spinning the long-drawn thread
> With backward steps. Yet ever as there passed
> A man whose garments shewed the soldier's red,
> Or crippled mendicant in sailor's garb,
> The little child who sat to turn the wheel
> Ceased from his toil, and she, with faltering voice,
> Expecting still to hear her husband's fate,
> Made many a fond inquiry; and when they
> Whose presence gave no comfort were gone by,
> Her heart was still more sad. And by yon gate
> That bars the traveller's road she often sat,
> And when a stranger-horseman came, the latch
> Would lift, and in his face look wistfully,
> Most happy if from aught discovered there
> Of tender feeling she might dare repeat

[1] At both the beginning and the end of the Preface, Wordsworth expresses the hope that his critical positions have enabled him to write a kind of poetry 'adapted to interest mankind permanently'.

> The same sad question.
>   Meanwhile her poor hut
> Sunk to decay; for he was gone, whose hand
> At the first nippings of October frost
> Closed up each chink, and with fresh bands of straw
> Chequered the green-grown thatch. And so she sat
> Through the long winter, reckless and alone,
> Till this reft house, by frost, and thaw, and rain,
> Was sapped; and when she slept, the nightly damps
> Did chill her breast, and in the stormy day
> Her tattered clothes were ruffled by the wind
> Even at the side of her own fire. Yet still
> She loved this wretched spot, nor would for worlds
> Have parted hence; and still that length of road,
> And this rude bench, one torturing hope endeared,
> Fast rooted at her heart. And, stranger, here
> In sickness she remained, and here she died,
> Last human tenant of these ruined walls.'[1]

The ruined walls, 'tenanted' now only by animals,[2] belong presumably to an actual cottage that Wordsworth and his sister Dorothy found near Racedown, in Dorset, where they were living in the early summer of 1797. Margaret, however, has a literary source: the brief vignette of a war-widow in Book VII of Southey's *Joan of Arc*, published the previous year. 'Yet did he leave behind', Southey had written of a soldier dying on the battlefield,

> One who did never say her daily prayers
> Of him forgetful; who to every tale
> Of the distant war lending an eager ear,
> Grew pale and trembled. At her cottage door
> The wretched one shall sit, and with dim eye
> Gaze o'er the plain, where on his parting steps
> Her last look hung.

'Nor ever shall she know', Southey adds,

> Her husband dead, but tortured with vain hope

---

[1] Lines 454–92, quoted in the earliest surviving version, transcribed by Dorothy for Coleridge on 10 June 1797, *Letters of Samuel Taylor Coleridge* ('Griggs' in future references), ed. E.L. Griggs (6 vols., Oxford, 1956–71), I, 327–8.

[2]
>   the unshod colt,
> The wandering heifer and the potter's ass,
> Find shelter now within the chimney-wall
> Where I have seen her evening hearthstone blaze . . .
>   (ll. 111–14)

> Gaze on – then, heart-sick, turn to her poor babe,
> And weep it fatherless.[1]

It must have been a common enough situation when Southey and Wordsworth were writing. The war with France had led to new taxes that fell especially on the poor, and a bad harvest in 1794 had pushed up the price of bread. Men had either enlisted, as Robert does in *The Ruined Cottage*, for the sake of the bounty, or been taken forcibly by the press-gang; and their wives would often not have known whether they were alive or dead. It is very much the material that Wordsworth had used in his own anti-war poem, *Salisbury Plain* (1793–5), and he accepts the story that is hinted at in Southey's lines without feeling the need to make significant changes. The major difference is one of attitude. Southey is making a political protest, but for Wordsworth the war is now almost irrelevant. *The Ruined Cottage* as he points out (rather priggishly) is 'a common tale / By moving accidents uncharactered' – a tale that is 'scarcely palpable / To him who does not think' (ll. 231–6). All the emphasis is on Margaret's states of mind, none on the plot. Those who are willing to think patiently 'into the human heart' will find the poetry full of beauty and power; those who are looking for a good story in a more obvious sense may well be disappointed.

Half-way through his account of the war-widow, Southey moves uncomfortably into the future tense ('At her cottage-door / The wretched one *shall* sit') – pathos is to be extracted from the fact that the woman's suffering is not yet over. Wordsworth instead puts his story firmly in the past, drawing on our sympathy for the dead, and introducing a new immediacy in the contrasts of past and present. The Pedlar who tells the story and the Poet who is his audience sit on the very cottage-bench where Margaret sat 'shaping things / Which made her heart beat quick' – the bench that had been endeared to her by the torturing hope of Robert's return. The desolation around them is the final stage of the story that is being told. We come to know Margaret through her surroundings. So much so, that in the description of her last years she seems almost to be merged with the cottage that is the visible symbol of her decline:

> 'Meanwhile her poor hut
> Sunk to decay; for he was gone, whose hand
> At the first nippings of October frost
> Closed up each chink, and with fresh bands of straw
> Chequered the green-grown thatch. And so she lived
> Through the long winter, reckless and alone,

[1] *Joan of Arc*, VII. 320–31. Wordsworth had certainly read Southey's poem, but may also have seen the lines about the war-widow reprinted in Coleridge's periodical, *The Watchman*, 1 March 1796.

> Till this reft house, by frost, and thaw, and rain,
> Was sapped; and when she slept, the nightly damps
> Did chill her breast . . . '
>   (ll. 476–84)

It is the cottage that sinks to decay, the cottage that is 'poor' and 'reft' (deprived), and missing Robert's attentions.

Of course, as one reads, sympathy is transferred from the cottage to Margaret, to whom it properly belongs. But when he goes on (or back) to write the beginning of his poem, Wordsworth carries with him this curiously strong sense of the cottage itself as having suffered. The Poet as he toils across the 'bare wide common' in the opening lines finds not an ordinary ruin, but 'four naked walls / That stared upon each other' (ll. 31–2). And the same emphasis on the cottage's painful vulnerability is apparent in the Pedlar's formal lament for Margaret:

>   'She is dead,
> The worm is on her cheek, and this poor hut,
> Stripped of its outward garb of houshold flowers,
> Of rose and sweetbriar, offers to the wind
> A cold bare wall whose earthy top is tricked
> With weeds and the rank speargrass.
>   (ll. 103–8)

The detail of the worm on Margaret's cheek is shockingly physical. Death is felt as a kind of sexual intrusion, and the poet's horror finds expression in his sense of the cottage as brutally stripped, and offering itself (almost it seems in a form of prostitution) to the wind.

In this reading, the weeds and speargrass seem a kind of tawdry finery in which the cottage decks itself, now that its decent original 'garb of houshold flowers' has been stripped away. But there are other ways of looking at Nature's 'silent overgrowings', and at the relation of Margaret to her surroundings. The Pedlar (who unobtrusively guides our reading, as he guides the Poet in his response) draws attention especially to a bond that has existed between Margaret's family and the waters of the well:

>   'Beside yon spring I stood,
> And eyed its waters till we seemed to feel
> One sadness, they and I. For them a bond
> Of brotherhood is broken: time has been
> When every day the touch of human hand
> Disturbed their stillness, and they ministered
> To human comfort. When I stooped to drink
> A spider's web hung to the water's edge,
> And on the wet and slimy foot-stone lay
> The useless fragment of a wooden bowl.'
>   (ll. 82–91)

The last lines sound so ordinary that one might not recognize the
pitcher broken at the fountain in Ecclesiastes, but there can be no
doubt that Wordsworth had in mind this archetypal image of life
stopped at its source.[1] In *An Evening Walk*, published in 1793, he had
made a far less subtle allusion:

> For Hope's deserted well why wistful look? –
> Choked is the pathway, and the pitcher broke.
>
> (ll. 255–6)

In *The Ruined Cottage* stilted metaphors have been replaced by a poetry
of everyday life. The deserted well of Hope becomes a real well, the
biblical pitcher is now the fragment of a drinking bowl used by
Margaret and her family, and the choking of the pathway too becomes
an observable detail: 'Seest thou that path? / The green-sward now has
broken its grey line' (ll. 457–8). But this movement away from the liter-
ary and artificial does not mean that the poetry is no longer symbolic;
it means that it is no longer obviously so. Wordsworth has found a way
of giving symbols strength by taking them back to their ordinariness.
More surprisingly he has also found a way of giving them life.

The bond between the waters of the well and Margaret's family
comes, as the poem progresses, to be seen as part of a more general
relationship between man and the natural forces amongst which he
lives. There is a balance to be preserved. Nature is active, and will
'minister to human comfort' only as long as it is met by countering
activity. Because the story begins at the end, we are first aware of the
balance – in the symbol of the bowl, and the desolation of the garden
– as having completely broken down. Then, as the Pedlar goes back to
record the different stages of Margaret's decline, it becomes clear that
Wordsworth has devised a peculiarly sensitive way of registering
emotional change, without the crudity of direct narrative ('She felt
this – she felt that').

The Ruined Cottage is built up around the four visits of the Pedlar to
Margaret after her husband's enlistment; but before moving on to her
story Wordsworth offers, as a sort of trailer, a brilliant study of the
effects of unemployment on Robert:

> 'his good humour soon
> Became a weight in which no pleasure was,

---

[1] See the great final chapter of Ecclesiastes, 'Remember now thy Creator in
the days of thy youth':

> Or ever the silver cord be loosed, or the
> golden bowl be broken, or the pitcher be broken
> at the fountain, or the wheel broken at the cistern.
>   Then shall the dust return to the earth as it
> was: and the spirit shall return unto God who gave it.

> And poverty brought on a petted mood
> And a sore temper. Day by day he drooped,
> And he would leave his home, and to the town
> Without an errand would he turn his steps,
> Or wander here and there among the fields.
> One while he would speak lightly of his babes
> And with a cruel tongue; at other times
> He played with them wild freaks of merriment,
> And 'twas a piteous thing to see the looks
> Of the poor innocent children. "Every smile",
> Said Margaret to me here beneath these trees,
> "Made my heart bleed." '
>
> (ll. 172–85)

The concept of good humour as a weight, the listlessness and alternation of Robert's moods, and especially the observation that it would be the children's smiles, not their sadness or perplexity, that were most painful – all show the extraordinary psychological insight that is to be found in these poems. And the passage is also beautifully handled from a structural point of view. In the long term it shows the rhythms of Robert's life breaking down under stress, as Margaret's will do later; in terms of an immediate effect, it creates for Margaret a sympathy that will be carried over into the main body of the poem. Most of the passage has not seemed to be about her at all, but in the final poignant moment of dialogue we become aware that she has been present throughout. It is she who has told the Pedlar what 'a piteous thing' it was to see the looks of 'the poor innocent children', she who has watched her husband going to pieces, suffered his petted moods and sore temper. The most important line in the passage is one that appears to be doing no work at all:

> ' "Every smile",
> *Said Margaret to me here beneath these trees*,
> "Made my heart bleed." '

Not only does the central line delay, and enhance, the effect of Margaret's statement, it brings home her emotion by reference to the trees that have seen it all, and lasted on. Their age and aloofness show up the littleness of the human lives beneath. And yet – as Wordsworth well understood – human feeling when associated with the permanence of Nature may be felt to take on some of the same abiding quality.[1]

---

[1] Wordsworth himself would go a lot further. He has, he says in the Preface to *Lyrical Ballads*, 'a deep impression of certain inherent and indestructible qualities of the human mind; and likewise of certain powers in the great and permanent objects [of Nature] that act upon it, which are equally inherent and indestructible'.

The first of the Pedlar's visits after Robert's enlistment finds Margaret grief-stricken and apparently without hope:

> 'With fervent love, and with a face of grief
> Unutterably helpless, and a look
> That seemed to cling upon me, she enquired
> If I had seen her husband.'
>
> (ll. 254–7)

She is, however, capable of greater resilience than he is himself (presumably he knows too much about the war), and together they 'build up a pile of better thoughts'. 'It was then the early spring', the Pedlar recalls, 'I left her busy with her garden tools.' It seems a casual recollection, but it isn't. Wordsworth has prepared the way for the accounts of Margaret's garden on which we come to depend in the Pedlar's succeeding visits:

> 'I came this way again
> Towards the wane of summer . . .
>
> In the shade,
> Where now we sit, I waited her return.
> Her cottage in its outward look appeared
> As chearful as before, in any shew
> Of neatness little changed – but that I thought
> The honeysuckle crowded round the door
> And from the wall hung down in heavier tufts,
> And knots of worthless stonecrop started out
> Along the window's edge, and grew like weeds
> Against the lower panes.'

'I turned aside', the Pedlar adds, 'And strolled into her garden. *It was changed*' (ll. 298–9, 303–13).

The distinction between cottage and garden is not really as marked in this case as Wordsworth's brief dramatic statement makes it sound. Active Nature that has been crowding unrestrained round Margaret's door has been at work in the garden too:

> 'The unprofitable bindweed spread his bells
> From side to side, and with unwieldy wreaths
> Had dragged the rose from its sustaining wall
> And bent it down to earth. The border tufts,
> Daisy, and thrift, and lowly camomile,
> And thyme, had straggled out into the paths
> Which they were used to deck.'
>
> (ll. 314–20)

On one level, of course, one can say that Margaret is unhappy, and so not getting on with her gardening. There can be little doubt, however, that Wordsworth saw the choking of the pathways in symbolic terms; and, in addition, it is surely tempting to see the rose, dragged from its sustaining wall, as an emblem of Margaret herself. As with the wooden bowl at the well, there is a concealed allusion – this time not to the Bible, but to *Paradise Lost*. Eve in Book IX, tending roses on her own after taking leave of Adam, is first described as 'stooping to support / Each flower of slender stalk, whose head . . . Hung drooping unsustained', and then referred to quite specifically as herself the 'fairest unsupported flower, / From her best prop so far . . . ' (ll. 427–33). Margaret's situation is very different of course. It is no fault of hers that 'her best prop' is so far away, and *The Ruined Cottage* contains no serpents or temptations– but the part played by gardening in the two poems remains curiously similar. In each case it represents happy and useful activity, and in each case it is held to be necessary; and yet in neither poem does it have an economic motive. One would surely expect Margaret's to be a vegetable-garden, but it isn't. The point comes through unexpectedly in Wordsworth's language: the bindweed is regarded as 'unprofitable', but is logically no more so than the rose which it has pulled down; and the reference to 'knots of *worthless* stonecrop' is odder still. The crime the knots have committed is to grow 'like weeds' against the window-panes. But by ordinary standards they *are* weeds. The implication seems to be that if the stonecrop were under control it could be accepted, perhaps even regarded as a flower. To be 'profitable', or 'worthy', is to fit into the total scheme of things – in effect, to be orderly.[1] Flowers that straggle out into paths 'which they were used to deck' are no more acceptable than weeds, because both equally symbolize the breaking down of harmony. As Eve puts it,

> what we by day
> Lop overgrown, or prune, or prop, or bind,
> One night or two with wanton growth derides,
> Tending to wild.
>> (*Paradise Lost*, IX. 209–12)

Because of the Fall, we never know if wildness could really have become a threat in Paradise – it hardly seems likely – but in *The Ruined Cottage* we are aware of it as the state that Margaret's garden reaches *at her death*:

> It was a plot
> Of garden-ground now wild, its matted weeds
> Marked with the steps of those whom as they passed,
> The gooseberry-trees that shot in long lank slips,
> Or currants hanging from their leafless stems

---

[1] Wordsworth seems later to have become aware of the more usual sense in which a garden could be 'profitable'; in *Excursion* Book I – the rose pulled from its sustaining walls becomes, by an unconscious pun, 'two small *rows* of peas'.

In scanty strings, had tempted to o'erleap
The broken wall.
(ll. 54–60)

On the Pedlar's third visit to the cottage, Margaret herself is 'sad and drooping'; her house bespeaks 'a sleepy hand of negligence'; her child has caught from her the 'trick' (habit) of grief, and sighs among its playthings. And yet such are the expectations that have been set up, that we take it for granted the garden will provide the deeper implications:

'Once again
I turned towards the garden-gate, and saw
More plainly still that poverty and grief
Were now come nearer to her. The earth was hard,
With weeds defaced and knots of withered grass;
No ridges there appeared of clear black mould,
No winter greenness. Of her herbs and flowers
It seemed the better part were gnawed away
Or trampled on the earth.'
(ll. 411–19)

There is no logical way in which a garden that has not been dug could tell us more of poverty and grief than an unhappy child. We accept that it does so because the different levels and suggestions of the poetry are working so powerfully together: Margaret too sad to dig; Margaret failing in her bond, and subject to 'the calm oblivious tendencies / Of Nature' (ll. 504–5) that will finally take over; Margaret suffering because in some curious sense she *is* her surroundings. The flowers that are gnawed away or trampled to the earth represent in all these ways a stage between the harmless, unpainful, encroachments of the honeysuckle and stonecrop, and the brutal last stripping of the household 'garb'. It is at this point that Wordsworth introduces the moving and beautiful symbol of the appletree, sharpening our awareness of suffering by bringing the merely implied grief into the presence of Margaret's actual pain:

'A chain of straw
Which had been twisted round the tender stem
Of a young appletree, lay at its root;
The bark was nibbled round by truant sheep.
Margaret stood near, her infant in her arms,
And, seeing that my eye was on the tree,
She said, "I fear it will be dead and gone
Ere Robert come again." '
(ll. 419–26)

Margaret thinks of the tree – indeed thinks of everything – in terms of Robert. We, on the other hand, see it in terms of Margaret herself, who of course we know will be 'dead and gone / Ere Robert come again'. It is the bringing together of these two kinds of response that creates this great moment of tragic poetry. The poem has reached a turning-point. Margaret seems utterly despairing; and yet from now on it is her hope not her suffering that will be stressed, because it is hope, persisting in the face of probability and logic, that has the sharper tragic implication. The account of Margaret's last years – dominated by her sad, earnest questioning of travellers, and the increasing decay of her cottage – brings Wordsworth to the place where he had started. The earliest versions of the poem were permitted to end blankly and without any attempt at a final consolation, 'and here she died, / Last human tenant of these ruined walls'. In March 1798, however, Wordsworth decided to add the beautiful reconciling image of the speargrass. 'Enough to sorrow have you given', the Pedlar says, addressing the Poet whose 'impotence of grief' for Margaret we are likely to share,

> 'The purposes of wisdom ask no more:
> Be wise and chearful, and no longer read
> The forms of things with an unworthy eye:
> She sleeps in the calm earth, and peace is here.
> I well remember that those very plumes,
> Those weeds, and the high speargrass on that wall,
> By mist and silent raindrops silvered o'er,
> As once I passed did to my mind convey
> So still an image of tranquility,
> So calm and still, and looked so beautiful
> Amid the uneasy thoughts which filled my mind,
> That what we feel of sorrow and despair
> From ruin and from change, and all the grief
> The passing shews of being leave behind,
> Appeared an idle dream that could not live
> Where meditation was. I turned away,
> And walked along my road in happiness.'
>   (ll. 508–25)

To be asked suddenly to think of Margaret's life as a 'passing *shew* of being' seems terribly harsh, and not everybody will be won over by talk of 'meditation' and 'the purposes of wisdom'. But the poetry does have a compelling tranquillity, and there is a special appropriateness in that consolation is offered in terms of the weeds and flowers that have been used throughout to tell the story. One may if one chooses take the speargrass, 'By mist and silent raindrops silvered o'er', to be another emblem of Margaret herself (like the rose and the appletree); but whether one does or not, it is a comfort to think of her as assimilated into the natural world – a part of the wildness that she was finally unable to check. Nor is the Pedlar's wisdom really so unacceptable. He is shown as making a very personal response to the story as he tells it, and he does not say that he is always capable of thinking dispassionately of human suffering – merely that on one occasion the beauty of the speargrass enabled him to do so.

Numerous small echoes suggest that Wordsworth began *The Brothers* at Christmas 1799 with *The Ruined Cottage* in mind. Because of the dramatic form he has now decided to use, the two poems appear very different; but Margaret's story had of course been told within the framework of a conversation, and for the high points Wordsworth had on several important occasions turned to dialogue. In terms of situation too, *The Brothers* seems more a development than a new beginning. Leonard and 'the homely priest of Ennerdale' meet, as the Poet and Pedlar had done, at a spot that prompts the telling of the story. The difference is that Leonard, instead of being the eventual narrator, is one of the principal characters in the story that he hears: in effect he is Robert returned to find out if Margaret is still alive. Because of this there is an element of suspense that is not present in *The Ruined Cottage*. But it is a very muted kind of suspense. The conversation takes place throughout beside James' grave; what we see is not Leonard discovering the fact of his brother's death, but the alternating moods of grief and self-deluding hope as he brings himself to accept it. In effect Wordsworth has once more begun his story at the end, and it is interesting that as with Margaret's cottage (and Michael's sheepfold), his actual starting-point was a relic from the past that had come to be symbolic of mortality.

On a walking-tour in the Lake District in November 1799, Wordsworth and Coleridge heard of the deaths of Jerome Bowman – who broke his leg near Scale Force, crawled three miles at night on hands and knees, and then died from his injuries – and his unnamed son, who, in the laconic words of Coleridge's notebook, 'broke his neck before this, by falling off a crag'. He was 'supposed', Coleridge goes on, 'to have layed down and slept, but walked in his sleep'; and then he adds the detail that especially appealed to Wordsworth's imagination: 'This was at Proud Knot on the mountain called Pillar up Ennerdale. His pike-staff stuck midway and stayed there till it rotted away.'[1] The courage and physical suffering of the elder Bowman did not seem to Wordsworth to be material for poetry; and the story he devised to incorporate the death of Bowman's son makes nothing of the event in its own right. *The Brothers* is about feelings and relation-

---

[1] *Notebooks of Samuel Taylor Coleridge*, ed. Kathleen Coburn (3 vols. so far, New York and London, 1957–) I, entry 540.

ship, about community and loneliness, and about the the different kinds of memorial that the dead may leave behind.

It is the wooden bowl found by the Pedlar at Margaret's well that James' staff most strongly recalls as it moulders half-way down the cliff. The staff, or crook, is an emblem of the shepherd's way of life, just as the bowl had represented Margaret's relationship to an outer world, in her giving of water to passers-by.[1] Both objects now are useless and in decay; but, surviving at the places where their owners died, they have come to be memorials – while they last, and while there is somebody there to recognize them. The Pedlar makes the point in lines that lead up to the discovery of the bowl:

> 'I see around me here
> Things which you cannot see. We die, my friend,
> Nor we alone, but that which each man loved
> And prized in his peculiar nook of earth
> Dies with him, or is changed, and very soon
> Even of the good is no memorial left.'
>
> (ll. 67–72)

Margaret has lived and died in isolation: there seems to be no adjacent village, and she has no bonds with the parish, or the nearby town, to which Robert at one point 'turns his steps' (ll. 175–7). Only the Pedlar remains who can 'see' the past amid the desolation of the present.[2] In this respect the situation in *The Brothers* is entirely different. Wordsworth sets his new poem in an ideal village community, of which the dead are effectively still members. As Leonard puts it to the Priest, 'Your dalesmen, then, do in each other's thoughts / Possess a kind of second life' (ll. 182–3). Gravestones are unnecessary because the dead are talked of by the fireside. Everybody knows who everybody was, and so no one can lack a memorial.

As part of the community, James has been 'the child of all the dale', lovingly supported while he lived, and lovingly remembered. Leonard too had once been part of it – indeed their 'bond of brotherhood' had seemed to typify all that was best in the dalesman's way of life (ll. 245–63) – but on his return after twenty years he is unrecognized, regarded as a tourist and a stranger, and even told his own story. He has of course only to say his name, and the church bells will carry the news of his homecoming from Ennerdale to Egremont. But he doesn't, because there is truly a sense in which he is a stranger, isolated by a depth of feeling that could be met perhaps in a reunion with James,

---

[1] The importance of Margaret's charity is discussed in *Music of Humanity* (London and New York, 1969), p. 128.
[2] To some extent the Poet becomes able to do so too, as a result of listening to the story (*Ruined Cottage*, 501–7).

but which cannot be softened down, rendered once again part of a general harmony. His hope has been too great, and his loss cannot be shared or contained. James in him will have a memorial of quite another kind.

We first become aware of the strength of Leonard's feelings in the curious account of his self-delusion over James' grave. He has come to the churchyard because he daren't enquire if his brother is still alive, and he has found the extra grave that tells him plainly of his death. Wordsworth's tones at this point are so bare and flat that they seem to say that the whole story is over. Then there is a change:

> but as he gazed there grew
> Such a confusion in his memory
> That he began to doubt, and he had hopes
> That he had seen this heap of turf before –
> That it was not another grave, but one
> He had forgotten.
>   (ll. 83–8)

We should be remembering by now that there had already been an example of what imagination can do aided by emotional need. During his twenty years at sea, Leonard not only heard 'The tones of water-falls and inland sounds' in the piping of the shrouds (ll. 44–5), but 'would often hang / Over the vessel's side, *and gaze and gaze*' till in the waves beneath him he

> Saw mountains, saw the forms of sheep that grazed
> On verdant hills, with dwellings among trees,
> And shepherds clad in the same country grey
> Which he himself had worn.
>   (ll. 51–2, 59–62)

In the churchyard the same abstracted gazing produces a sort of 'calenture' of false hope.[1] Recollecting an occasion during the day when he has in fact misremembered a detail from the past, Leonard becomes so exalted that he imagines 'the rocks, / And the eternal hills themselves, [are] changed' (ll. 95–6). There is a playfulness now in Wordsworth's voice – a sort of tender mockery of the mortal who thinks he can see change amid the permanent forms of Nature – but there is admiration too, for the power of love that is implied in such wilful self-deluding.

There is one part of the landscape in which Leonard is right to see a change. 'Aye, there indeed your memory is a friend', the Priest comments,

---

[1] The 'calenture' is correctly a disease of the tropics in which sailors leap over-board in the delusion that they see green fields, but Wordsworth uses it as a sort of mirage at sea. For the source of his description, see Notes, below.

> That does not play you false. On that tall pike
> (It is the loneliest place of all these hills)
> There were two springs which bubbled side by side
> As if they had been made that they might be
> Companions for each other!
>
> (ll. 135–40)

Memory as a friend; springs as companions; and a few lines earlier
Leonard has referred to the dalesman's quiet life in which the 'years
make up *one peaceful family*' – *The Brothers* is for Wordsworth unusually
rich in figurative writing, and especially important are the images of
relationship that reflect on the poet's central theme.[1] 'Ten years back',
the Priest continues,

> Close to *those brother fountains*, the huge crag
> Was rent with lightning – one is dead and gone,
> The other, left behind, is flowing still.
>
> (ll. 140–3)

Not only do we know of Leonard and James as the brothers of the
poem's title, we have heard them referred to as 'brother shepherds';
given the Priest's humanizing elegiac language ('one is dead and
gone'), we are not likely to miss an allusion in the 'brother fountains'
that seem as if they were made to be companions to each other. Less
obvious is the way the lines are working in dramatic terms. *We* know
that the dead fountain is James; but for Leonard, the Priest's words, if
they are assimilated, must be a source of futile hope. After twenty
years the Priest would be likely to think of Leonard as dead; it is James
who has been 'left behind', and should be 'flowing still'.

We can't be certain that Wordsworth intended this effect, but *The
Brothers* is a carefully made poem, and it seems entirely probable. The
Priest, with his self-pleasure and his good heart, is a far more sophis-
ticated creation than the Pedlar. For much of the poem his garrulous-
ness convincingly prevents the fact of James' death emerging, and
when Leonard does manage to ask a straight question, he doesn't get
an answer:

LEONARD It seems these brothers have not lived to be
　　　　　A comfort to each other?
PRIEST　　　　　　　　　　　　That they might
　　　　　Live to that end, is what both old and young
　　　　　In this our valley all of us have wished –
　　　　　And what, for my part, I have often prayed.
　　　　　But Leonard . . .

---

[1] In retrospect one may notice, for instance, the pair of combs which at
ll. 32–3 the Priest lays 'with gentle care, / Each in the other locked' – as
Leonard and James can never be.

LEONARD   Then James still is left among you?
PRIEST   'Tis of the elder brother I am speaking.
                     They had an uncle . . .
                              (ll. 281–8)

Alongside the tension in the dialogue that comes from Leonard's hope
– or from his need to be allowed to hope – there is the reader's growing
wish for him to tell the Priest who he is. Once or twice it seems that he
may have given himself away by showing more knowledge than a
stranger could have possessed; but in fact of course he can neither be
permitted to reveal himself, nor be unmasked, because without James
a joyful homecoming is unthinkable. And so the poem moves on to its
conclusion, in which Leonard, unable to rejoin the community of the
past, or come to terms with his grief, goes back without hope to the
sea. For him the rocks and the eternal hills have indeed been changed.

  The Brothers, however, contains more of consolation than either *The
Ruined Cottage* or *Michael*. Though he cannot reveal himself to the
Priest, Leonard is allowed to set things straight by letter after he has
left the village, and for the reader it is a very welcome concession. He
also of course outlives the poem, as Margaret and Michael cannot,
and the detail of his being '*now* / A seaman, a grey-headed mariner' (ll.
430–1) to some extent takes the edge off his grief. Most important,
though, is the use that Wordsworth makes of Bowman's staff. James
falls from the crag, is found 'Dead, and with mangled limbs' (l. 378),
and duly buried. Leonard is reassured that his brother has not com-
mitted suicide, and the poet quietly introduces the symbol that had
been his starting-point:

        We guess that in his hands he must have had
        His shepherd's staff; for midway in the cliff
        It had been caught, and *there* for many years
        It hung – and mouldered *there*.
                              (ll. 399–402)

The tones of the verse, the break that occurs at this point in the poem,
and especially the repetition of the word 'there', bring Margaret's
death vividly to mind:

                      'And *here*, my friend,
        In sickness she remained; and *here* she died,
        Last human tenant of these ruined walls.'

Consciously or otherwise, Wordsworth is patterning himself on the
original ending of *The Ruined Cottage*.[1] But where the naked, staring
walls of Margaret's house bring associations only of pain, the survival
of the staff seems oddly consoling. The Priest may take pleasure in
James' decent burial, but the comfort offered to the rest of us is that

[1]See Notes, below.

the staff has lasted on, peaceful and undisturbed, until in the fullness of time it rotted away. In its power to assuage it is closer to the spear-grass, 'By mist and silent raindrops silvered o'er', than it is to the cottage. Visible, and yet out of reach – midway in the cliff; and mid-way, in effect, between life and death – it confers upon James a sort of half-life of the imagination.

Coleridge described *The Ruined Cottage* as 'the finest poem in our language, comparing it with any of the same or similar length', and referred to *The Brothers* as 'that model of English pastoral, which I have never yet read with unclouded eye'.[1] There are ways in which *Michael* is still more impressive. Once again Wordsworth seems to have started writing with a particular symbol in mind. 'After dinner', Dorothy records in her *Journal* on 11 October 1800, 'we walked up Greenhead Gill in search of a sheepfold.' Clearly it was a particular fold which the poet had noticed already; and like both the cottage and the staff, it was in a state of decay. As Wordsworth put it, in some beautiful lines that were not used in the final poem:

> There is a shapeless crowd of unhewn stones
> That lie together, some in heaps, and some
> In lines, that seem to keep themselves alive
> In the last dotage of a dying form.[2]

Dorothy comments that the sheepfold is 'falling away', and then adds a detail that seems prophetic of the poem that her brother will write: 'it is built nearly in the form of a heart unequally divided'.

Like the ruined cottage, the sheepfold makes its appearance at the very beginning of the poem. Wordsworth's tones in introducing it, however, are much less relaxed. After his experiment with dialogue he has returned to direct narrative, and addresses the reader in a rather hearty version of his own voice:

> If from the public way you turn your steps
> Up the tumultuous brook of Greenhead Gill
> You will suppose that with an upright path
> Your feet must struggle . . .
> But courage! . . .
>   (ll. 1–6)

---

[1] Coleridge to Lady Beaumont, 3 April 1815 (Griggs, IV, 564), and *Biographia Literaria*, ed. George Watson (Everyman's Library, London, 1956), chapter XVIII, 217n.

[2] *Poetical Works of William Wordsworth*, ed. E. de Selincourt and Helen Darbishire, Oxford, 1940–9 ('*Oxford Wordsworth*' in future references), II, 482; Wordsworth wrote a great deal for *Michael* that was not included in the printed poem. For other memorable passages from the drafts, see notes to ll. 13–17 and 62–4, below.

The magical image of the stones keeping themselves alive in the dying form of the sheepfold perhaps seemed to draw too much attention to itself. Wordsworth at any rate discards it, giving us instead a little nudge about how to read his poem:

> Beside the brook
> There is a straggling heap of unhewn stones;
> And to that place a story appertains,
> Which, *though it be ungarnished with events*,
> Is not unfit, I deem, for the fireside
> Or for the summer shade.
> (ll. 16–21)

As in *The Ruined Cottage*, Wordsworth is telling us that his is 'a common tale / By moving accidents uncharactered', but he has a new motive now since coming back to live in the Lake District.

In January 1801, Wordsworth sent a copy of the two-volume *Lyrical Ballads* to the Whig Leader of the Opposition in the House of Commons, Charles James Fox, drawing his attention especially to *The Brothers* and *Michael*. 'I have attempted', he writes,

to draw a picture of the domestic affections as I know they exist amongst a class of men who are now almost confined to the North of England. They are small independent *proprietors* of land, here called 'statesmen' – men of respectable education who daily labour on their own little properties. 'The domestic affections', he continues,

will always be strong amongst men who live in a country not crowded with population, if these men are placed above poverty. But if they are proprietors of small estates which have descended to them from their ancestors, the power which these affections will acquire amongst such men is inconceivable by those who have only had an opportunity of observing hired labourers, farmers, and the manufacturing poor . . . This class of men is rapidly disappearing.

> (*EY*, 314–15)

Wordsworth was in fact trying to do several things at once. He was making a political point about the virtues of Lake District statesmen (such as Walter Ewbank of *The Brothers*, and Michael); he was trying in more general terms 'to shew that men who do not wear fine cloaths can feel deeply' (*EY*, 315); and he was, as ever, writing a poetry of the human heart, in which politics and class were finally irrelevant.

Michael, great poem though it is, is very slow to get under way. Wordsworth is too obviously conscious of his mission. In *The Brothers* the virtues of the people of Ennerdale had emerged through the dialogue and the Priest's self-pleasure – *his* parishioners would surely be willing to reap an acre of their neighbour's corn – but *Michael* has no Priest, or Pedlar, to take responsibility for the poet's views. The first half of the poem reads like a celebration of the statesman's way of life.

Long daylight hours on the fells tending to the sheep are sup-
plemented by night-time work, carding and spinning wool around the
lamp which has given the family its reputation, and the cottage its
name – the Evening Star:

> Early at evening did it burn, and late,
> Surviving comrade of uncounted hours
> Which going by from year to year had found
> And left the couple neither gay perhaps
> Nor chearful, yet with objects and with hopes
> Living a life of eager industry.
>
> (ll. 119–24)

After the very realistic, and not very attractive, detail of the couple's
lack of cheerfulness, the '*eager* industry' sounds false, and a little con-
descending. In Donne's phrase, Michael and Isabel are reduced to
'country ants'.[1] There are of course moments of unforced imaginative
poetry in the first part of *Michael*: the descriptions of the hidden valley,
for instance, where 'The mountains have all opened out themselves'
(l. 7), and of the shepherd on the fells,

> he had been alone
> Amid the heart of many thousand mists
> That came to him and left him on the heights.
>
> (ll. 58–60)

But two lines after this last numinous passage, we hear Wordsworth's
voice stridently proclaiming,

> *And grossly that man errs* who should suppose
> That the green valleys, and the streams and rocks,
> Were things indifferent to the shepherd's thoughts.
>
> (ll. 62–4)

Wordsworth needed to believe that Michael would be responsive to
the natural world about him, because in general he wished to portray
the statesman's life as an ideal. But for the purposes of his poem, the
green valleys were to be seen, and loved, chiefly as inherited land – a
guarantee of the shepherd's independence. The central conflict of the
poem was explained by Wordsworth in April 1801 to Thomas Poole,
the Somerset farmer who had to some extent been a model for Michael
himself:

In the last poem of my second volume I have attempted to give a picture
of a man of strong mind and lively sensibility, agitated by two of the most
powerful affections of the human heart: the parental affection, and the
love of property, *landed* property, including the feelings of inheritance,
home, and personal and family independence.

> (*EY*, 322)

---

[1] *The Sunne Rising*, 8.

Unlike *The Ruined Cottage* and *The Brothers*, *Michael* is a tragedy of choice. Margaret and Leonard are blameless in their suffering; Michael to some extent is the cause of his. Because of his age, dignity, and passionate integrity of life, it is difficult to think of him as wrong; but when he says, at the central moment in the poem, 'Heaven forgive me, Luke, / If I judge ill for thee' (ll. 389–90), there can be no doubt that he has done so. Too strongly identified with his land, he has attempted a compromise, when he might – and probably *should* – have responded wholly in terms of his love for Luke. As a result, he loses what is truly most important, and dies in tragic awareness of the mistake that he has made. And yet he has the entire sympathy of the poet, not just in his later suffering, but also in making the wrong decision.

Though isolated and ideal in its different way, the pastoral world of Wordsworth is not protected, as its more literary predecessors had been, from commercial realities. Walter Ewbank and Michael both inherit land that is heavily mortgaged. Walter dies under the burden; Michael pays off his original debt, but then offers a guarantee to his nephew, and suddenly in old age finds that his bond has been called in. His response is dignified and extremely sad:

> 'Isabel', said he,
> Two evenings after he had heard the news,
> 'I have been toiling more than seventy years,
> And in the open sunshine of God's love
> Have we all lived, yet if these fields of ours
> Should pass into a stranger's hand, I think
> That I could not lie quiet in my grave.'
> (ll. 236–42)

The last statement has an almost pedantic carefulness that increases its poignancy: the land, of course, *will* pass into a stranger's hand, and Michael will have no option but to lie quiet in his grave. Wordsworth catches beautifully too the confusions involved in the moment of wrong decision:

> 'When I began, my purpose was to speak
> Of remedies, and of a chearful hope.
> Our Luke shall leave us, Isabel; the land
> Shall not go from us, and it shall be free –
> He shall possess it, free as is the wind
> That passes over it.'
> (ll. 252–7)

Michael's intention is that Luke shall be away only for the time it takes to earn the necessary money; he can then come back to enjoy his inheritance. Through excited rhythms and jumbled trains of thought, however, Wordsworth has been able to suggest that Michael's priorities are far more confused than he knows. Luke's departure is seized on too eagerly as a remedy and cheerful hope, and the parallelism of 'Our Luke shall leave us' / 'The land shall not go from us' is there to suggest what exactly it is that is going wrong. The poetry is saying loudly and clearly that Luke and the land are alternatives. Not recognizing this, Michael temporarily values the land more highly than his son. That is to say, because he thinks he is going to lose it, he not unnaturally gives it more thought than he gives to Luke, in whom he feels secure. That this should matter is tragically unfair, but it does. In some ways Michael's next statement, or clause, is more telling even than the balancing of Luke and land. We expect 'The land shall not go from us' to be followed by 'and Luke will soon come back to enjoy it'; but the line of course continues, 'and *it* shall be free'. Even when Luke does again become the centre of his father's thoughts, and the subject of his sentence ('*He* shall possess it, free as is the wind / That passes over it'), the adjective 'free', which seems to be his by right, turns out to belong once more to the land. Wordsworth is not merely thinking into the human heart, he is portraying its confusions with extraordinary skill.

The land has been the centre of Michael's life, and of the life of his fathers; properly it should one day be the centre of Luke's. One way of looking at Michael's position is to say that it is in fact possible for him to value Luke above the land, because the two are not in his mind distinct. It is in terms of the land that he values both himself and his son. Luke exists as its next possessor. 'Here they lived', says Michael of his own parents,

> 'As all their forefathers had done; and when
> At length their time was come, they were not loth
> To give their bodies to the family mold.
> I wished that thou should'st live the life they lived;'
>
> (ll. 376–80)

Luke was born to be the continuation of a line – 'thou art the same / That wert a promise to me ere thy birth' (ll. 342–3) – and without the land he could not be so. Michael can scarcely be said to have had a choice. Both his decision and his tragedy seem fated.

We are never told how much Michael himself has understood. Our first information about his feelings comes from Isabel, who has herself inferred it not from anything that Michael says but from his movements in his sleep. One is reminded of the sighs which in *The Ruined Cottage* come on the Pedlar's ear from no apparent source (ll. 385–7). It is a beautiful example of Wordsworth's dealings in implication and indirection, and far more moving than any form of outright statement could have been. But it doesn't of course tell us the nature of Michael's sufferings. Isabel, who (in Wordsworth's rather condescending phrase from *The Prelude*) is 'wise, as women are', assumes that he is grieving straightforwardly over Luke's departure:

> 'Thou must not go,
> We have no other child but thee to lose,
> None to remember – do not go away,
> For if thou leave thy father he will die.'
>
> (ll. 304–7)

It is possible, however, to read the signs as implying not merely grief, but anxiety over the decision that has been taken; and in the great central episode of the laying of the corner-stone, we are encouraged to do so.

The final stages of the poem move from the cottage to the sheepfold – or to the site of the sheepfold – beside the boisterous brook of Greenhead Ghyll. There Michael, whose impressiveness seems more and more to recall the Old Testament, arranges a formal leave-taking, and binds Luke to a covenant:

> ' 'tis a long time to look back, my son,
> And see so little gain from sixty years.
> These fields were burthened when they came to me;
> Till I was forty years of age, not more
> Than half of my inheritance was mine.
> I toiled and toiled; God blessed me in my work,
> And till these three weeks past the land was free –
> It looks as if it never could endure
> Another master. Heaven forgive me, Luke,
> If I judge ill for thee, but it seems good
> That thou should'st go.'
>
> (ll. 381–91)

Earlier, Michael had felt he could not lie quiet in his grave if the land passed into the hand of a stranger; now, as his own emotions become stronger and more confused, the land itself is felt to rebel at the thought. More than half conscious of judging ill for Luke, Michael makes with him a strange bond which seems to be designed above all to assuage his own anxieties:

> 'I will begin again
> With many tasks that were resigned to thee;
> Up to the heights, and in among the storms,
> Will I without thee go again, and do
> All works which I was wont to do alone
> Before I knew thy face . . .
>
> but I forget
> My purposes. Lay now the corner-stone
> As I requested, and hereafter, Luke,
> When thou art gone away, should evil men
> Be thy companions, let this sheepfold be

> Thy anchor and thy shield. Amid all fear,
> And all temptation, let it be to thee
> An emblem of the life thy fathers lived . . .
>   Now, fare thee well.
> When thou return'st, thou in this place wilt see
> A work which is not here. A covenant
> 'Twill be between us – but whatever fate
> Befall thee, I shall love thee to the last,
> And bear thy memory with me to the grave.'
>   (ll. 401–6, 412–19, 421–6)

Ritual is not at all common in Wordsworth's poetry, and it is worth asking what has been achieved by the solemnity of this moment. From Michael's point of view, the covenant is a way of sharing still with Luke in the building of the fold which they had been going to do together – and, by an extension, a means of sharing in the larger task that Luke has been sent to London to accomplish. But it is more than this. A sort of magic is going on – a claiming of Luke. In laying the corner-stone, he dedicates himself to the way of life that his fathers have led. The fold is to be for him what Nature had been for the poet of *Tintern Abbey*, 'the anchor of [his] purest thoughts'. All this must one feels have Wordsworth's sympathy; and yet, as an emblem and protection the sheepfold proves to be useless. We know no details, but Luke clearly yields to temptation despite the powers it should have had. As in his original decision, Michael is attempting in the covenant to have things both ways – to keep Luke, though sending him away – and his magic cannot be successful. In the parallel that many readers feel between Michael and Luke, Abraham and Isaac, there may even be a hint of the ritual turning to sacrifice: Luke sacrificed to his father's gods.

Michael, it may be thought, attempts by the sheepfold to ratify his own mistake, claiming Luke as a partner in the wrong decision that has been made, by dedicating him to the very preoccupation that has been its cause. But not everybody will wish to read the poem in this way. Looked at from another point of view, the covenant is akin to Margaret's bond with waters of the well. Michael's stones are not alive like Margaret's flowers – the most they can do is 'straggle' – and the sheepfold is not used, as the garden is, to mark progressive stages of decline. At the end of the poem, however, the fold enables Wordsworth to form a tragic conclusion that neither *The Ruined Cottage* nor *The Brothers* can match.

Michael's foreboding words, 'but whatever fate / Befall thee, I shall love thee to the last', tell the reader what to expect, but not how the poet is to bring his poem to a climax. In the event, Luke is shuffled off to his 'hiding-place beyond the seas' (l. 456) with rather disgraceful speed, leaving Wordsworth free to tell us of Michael's final years. 'There is a comfort in the strength of love', he begins, quietly saying the opposite of what we should expect,

> 'Twill make a thing endurable which else
> Would break the heart – old Michael found it so.
> I have conversed with more than one who well
> Remember the old man, and what he was
> Years after he had heard this heavy news.
> His bodily frame had been from youth to age
> Of an unusual strength. Among the rocks
> He went, and still looked up upon the sun,
> And listened to the wind, and, as before,
> Performed all kinds of labour for his sheep
> And for the land, his small inheritance.
> And to that hollow dell from time to time
> Did he repair, to build the fold of which
> His flock had need.
>> (ll. 456–70)

The poetry seems to be telling us again and again that Michael is all right. The strength of his love (which one might have thought would be painful) is felt as a comfort; the loss of Luke (which should have been heart-breaking) is seen merely as an endurable *thing*; eye-witnesses testify to his having lived on for years, not only strong as ever, but also sensitive and industrious; at times, it seems, he was even capable of going to work at the sheepfold. But underneath all this, one feels the *need* for comfort – the resilience that it took to survive the heart-break and to go on living all that time according to the standards of the past. A series of allusions take us back into the poem, and bring out an especial poignancy. The reference to Michael's bodily frame repeats exactly lines 43–4 (except that we didn't know then how the unusual strength would finally be tested). The moving thought that Michael '*still* looked up upon the sun, / And listened to the wind' (refusing to be bowed) has behind it not just the days when he had seemed to live 'in the open sunshine of God's love' (l. 239), and 'learned the meaning of all winds' (l. 48), but a specific allusion to companionship with Luke:

> from the boy there came
> Feelings and emanations, *things which were*
> *Light to the sun and music to the wind* . . .
>> (ll. 210–12)

The lines that follow are packed with implications – Wordsworth nowhere writes with more feeling and control. Michael performing all kinds of labour for his sheep, and for the land, recalls his tender services to the infant Luke (ll. 162–8); and the fact that they are still '*his* sheep', and the land is '*his* small inheritance' (he is eighty-four), brings the grief of Luke's absence that much closer to the mind. Finally there is 'that hollow dell' to which

> from time to time
> [He did] repair, to build the fold of which
> His flock had need.

It is the poet's *not* referring to the covenant that brings it so strongly to the mind (it is neither here nor there whether the flock has need). ' 'Tis not forgotten yet', Wordsworth continues, at last conceding Michael's ordinary humanity,

> The pity which was then in every heart
> For the old man; and 'tis believed by all
> That many and many a day he thither went,
> And never lifted up a single stone.
> (ll. 470–4)

Michael will love Luke to the last, and bear his memory with him to the grave, but he cannot finish the sheepfold that was his own part in the covenant. To have completed the building would have been a sort of restitution to Luke – perhaps even a sort of justification for Michael himself. Neither, in this sternly tragic poem, can be permitted. Michael too fails in his bond. It is in his failure, however, that we feel the greatness of his love.

THE RUINED COTTAGE

First Part

'Twas Summer and the sun was mounted high;
Along the south the uplands feebly glared
Through a pale steam, and all the northern downs,
In clearer air ascending, shewed far off
Their surfaces with shadows dappled o'er   5
Of deep embattled clouds. Far as the sight
Could reach those many shadows lay in spots
Determined and unmoved, with steady beams
Of clear and pleasant sunshine interposed –   *re-reading*
Pleasant to him who on the soft cool moss   10
Extends his careless limbs beside the root
Of some huge oak whose aged branches make

1   In its brief original form, which does not survive, *The Ruined Cottage* was
read to Coleridge on 5 June 1797, and described by Dorothy as
'William's new poem' (*EY*, 189). Wordsworth may have gone on work-
ing on it during the summer, but his major revisions belong to
February–March 1798. The poem was then lengthened, and given a
more formal structure, by the addition of the opening section (ll. 1–54),
the central transition (ll. 185–237), and the final lines of reconciliation
(ll. 493–538). At the same time Wordsworth inserted under Coleridge's
influence a long philosophical account of the narrator's upbringing
which, though highly important in its own right, had the effect of
unbalancing the poem. Wordsworth therefore took it out again, and
until 1804 (when he drew up his scheme for *The Excursion*) the narrator's
history was regarded as a separate work, *The Pedlar*. *The Ruined Cottage*
meanwhile was left as the compact and tightly constructed poem
printed in this volume.

2–6 When creating an introduction (ll. 1–54) for *The Ruined Cottage*,
Wordsworth drew heavily on revisions made in 1794 to his early
descriptive poem *An Evening Walk* (written 1787–9, published 1793). To
form *Ruined Cottage*, 2–6, he merely rewrote as blank verse two existing
couplets:

> When in the south the wan noon brooding still
> Breathed a pale steam around the glaring hill,
> And on the northern hills in clearer air
> The shades of deep embattled clouds appear
> (*Oxford Wordsworth*, 1. 8, ll. 53–6 in revised text)

A twilight of their own, a dewy shade
Where the wren warbles while the dreaming man,
Half-conscious of that soothing melody,
With side-long eye looks out upon the scene,
By those impending branches made more soft,
More soft and distant.
                                Other lot was mine.
Across a bare wide common I had toiled
With languid feet which by the slippery ground
Were baffled still; and when I stretched myself
On the brown earth my limbs from very heat
Could find no rest, nor my weak arm disperse
The insect host which gathered round my face
And joined their murmurs to the tedious noise
Of seeds of bursting gorse that crackled round.
I rose and turned towards a group of trees
Which midway in that level stood alone;
And thither come at length, beneath a shade
Of clustering elms that sprang from the same root
I found a ruined house, four naked walls

17–18   The observation that distance is softened when seen through
         'impending branches' (ones that hang between the viewer and the land-
         scape) had a special importance for Wordsworth. Looking back he
         associated his original decision to become a poet with the moment
         when aged about fourteen he first noticed this effect.

18   **lot** fate.

19–26   Written as couplets in 1794 to be inserted after *Evening Walk*, 56:
                 When he who long with languid steps had toiled
                 Across the slippery moor oppressed and foiled
                 Sinks down and finds no rest, while as he turns
                 The fervid earth his languid body burns,
                 Nor can his weak arm faintly lifted chase
                 The insect host that gather round his face
                 And join their murmurs to the tedious sound
                 Of seeds of bursting furze that crackle round
                               (*Oxford Wordsworth*, I. 8)

29–30   Until the arrival of the Dutch-elm disease in the mid 1970s, elms were
         the chief feature of the southern English landscape. As Wordsworth
         points out, they sprang from suckers coming from a single root that ran
         along the hedgerows. They were therefore very numerous, and often
         beautifully grouped. See the paintings of Salisbury Cathedral and
         Dedham Vale by Wordsworth's contemporary, Constable.

31–2   The 'naked' walls, emphasizing the vulnerability of the cottage, were
         an afterthought. Wordsworth's original draft stressed rather the deso-

That stared upon each other. I looked round,
And near the door I saw an aged man
Alone and stretched upon the cottage bench;
An iron-pointed staff lay at his side.   35
With instantanious joy I recognized
That pride of Nature and of lowly life,
The venerable Armytage, a friend
As dear to me as is the setting sun.
           Two days before   40
We had been fellow-travellers. I knew
That he was in this neighbourhood, and now
Delighted found him here in the cool shade.
He lay, his pack of rustic merchandize
Pillowing his head. I guess he had no thought   45
Of his way-wandering life. His eyes were shut,
The shadows of the breezy elms above
Dappled his face. With thirsty heat oppressed
At length I hailed him, glad to see his hat
Bedewed with water-drops, as if the brim   50
Had newly scooped a running stream. He rose
And pointing to a sun-flower, bade me climb
The [   ] wall where that same gaudy flower

> lation and inhospitality of the place:
> I found a ruined cottage, four clay walls
> That stared upon each other. 'Twas a spot
> The wandering gypsey in a stormy night
> Would pass it with his moveables to house
> On the open plain beneath the imperfect arch
> Of a cold lime-kiln. As I looked round . . .
>
> (*Butler*, 44, ll. 30–5)

36–9 In the original *Ruined Cottage* of summer 1797 the Pedlar had addressed the poet as 'stranger' (see Introduction, p. 4 above), and Margaret's story had been one of unrelieved sadness. By February 1798, however, Wordsworth had decided to use the Pedlar as a spokesman for his own new optimistic philosophy, and he made the two men friends as a way of increasing the reader's confidence.

40 A defective line in the manuscript, as is l. 53 below.

44–6 'Did Mr Wordsworth really imagine', writes Francis Jeffrey in his very hostile review of *The Excursion* (1814), 'that his favourite doctrines were likely to gain any thing . . . by being put into the mouth of a person accustomed to higgle about tape, or brass sleeve-buttons?' He goes on to make the very reasonable point that nothing the Pedlar says or does has any reference to his 'low occupation'.

rustic merchandize goods for sale to country people.

Looked out upon the road.
                              It was a plot
Of garden-ground now wild, its matted weeds
Marked with the steps of those whom as they passed,
The gooseberry-trees that shot in long lank slips,
Or currants hanging from their leafless stems
In scanty strings, had tempted to o'erleap
The broken wall. Within that cheerless spot,
Where two tall hedgerows of thick alder boughs
Joined in a damp cold nook, I found a well
Half covered up with willow-flowers and grass.
I slaked my thirst and to the shady bench
Returned, and while I stood unbonneted
To catch the motion of the cooler air
The old man said, 'I see around me here
Things which you cannot see. We die, my friend,
Nor we alone, but that which each man loved
And prized in his peculiar nook of earth
Dies with him, or is changed, and very soon
Even of the good is no memorial left.
The poets, in their elegies and songs
Lamenting the departed, call the groves,
They call upon the hills and streams to mourn,
And senseless rocks – nor idly, for they speak
In these their invocations with a voice
Obedient to the strong creative power
Of human passion. Sympathies there are
More tranquil, yet perhaps of kindred birth,
That steal upon the meditative mind
And grow with thought. Beside yon spring I stood,
And eyed its waters till we seemed to feel
One sadness, they and I. For them a bond
Of brotherhood is broken: time has been
When every day the touch of human hand
Disturbed their stillness, and they ministered
To human comfort. When I stooped to drink
A spider's web hung to the water's edge,

75–9   Projection of human feelings onto 'senseless rocks' – the 'pathetic
       fallacy' that Nature cares, and is capable of grief – is justified for
       Wordsworth not because Nature *does* mourn, but because of the love
       and imagination shown in the wish that she could do so.

77   **invocations**   poetic addresses – literally, 'callings-upon'.

And on the wet and slimy foot-stone lay   90
The useless fragment of a wooden bowl.
It moved my very heart.
                              The day has been
When I could never pass this road but she
Who lived within these walls, when I appeared,
A daughter's welcome gave me, and I loved her   95
As my own child. Oh sir, the good die first,
And they whose hearts are dry as summer dust
Burn to the socket. Many a passenger
Has blessed poor Margaret for her gentle looks
When she upheld the cool refreshment drawn   100
From that forsaken spring, and no one came
But he was welcome, no one went away
But that it seemed she loved him. She is dead,
The worm is on her cheek, and this poor hut,
Stripped of its outward garb of household flowers,   105
Of rose and sweetbriar, offers to the wind
A cold bare wall whose earthy top is tricked
With weeds and the rank speargrass. She is dead,
And nettles rot and adders sun themselves
Where we have sate together while she nursed   110
Her infant at her breast. The unshod colt,
The wandering heifer and the potter's ass,
Find shelter now within the chimney-wall
Where I have seen her evening hearthstone blaze
And through the window spread upon the road   115
Its chearful light. You will forgive me, sir,

90–1   For Wordsworth's allusion at this point to the 'pitcher . . . broken at the
        fountain' (Ecclesiastes, 12.6), see Introduction, p. 7 above.
  98   **passenger**   passer-by.
104–8   Compare Goldsmith's *Deserted Village* (1770), 47–8:
                Sunk are thy bowers in shapeless ruin all,
                And the long grass o'ertops the mouldering wall
        Though direct borrowings are comparatively few, Goldsmith is pro-
        bably the most important influence on Wordsworth's narrative
        technique in *The Ruined Cottage*. For his narrator, as for the Pedlar,
        details of a now uninhabited landscape act as constant and painful
        reminders of a happy and industrious past.
 107   **tricked**   decked.
 116   Wordsworth's great final image of the speargrass (ll. 510–25, below) was
        originally to have been inserted at this point. The Pedlar was to have
        accused himself, not the listening poet, of reading 'The forms of things

But often on this cottage do I muse
As on a picture, till my wiser mind
Sinks, yielding to the foolishness of grief.
  She had a husband, an industrious man, *another stanza*
Sober and steady. I have heard her say
That he was up and busy at his loom
In summer ere the mower's scythe had swept
The dewy grass, and in the early spring
Ere the last star had vanished. They who passed
At evening, from behind the garden-fence
Might hear his busy spade, which he would ply
After his daily work till the daylight
Was gone, and every leaf and flower were lost
In the dark hedges. So they passed their days
In peace and comfort, and two pretty babes
Were their best hope next to the God in heaven.
  You may remember, now some ten years gone,
Two blighting seasons when the fields were left
With half a harvest. It pleased heaven to add
A worse affliction in the plague of war;
A happy land was stricken to the heart –
'Twas a sad time of sorrow and distress.
A wanderer among the cottages,
I with my pack of winter raiment saw
The hardships of that season. Many rich
Sunk down as in a dream among the poor,
And of the poor did many cease to be,
And their place knew them not. Meanwhile, abridged
Of daily comforts, gladly reconciled

with an unworthy eye': 'But *I* have spoken thus / With an ungrateful temper, and have read . . . '

133–8 England had been at war with France for four-and-a-half years when Wordsworth was writing, and there is no doubt that he had the contemporary situation in mind (the bad harvests of ll. 134–5, for instance, coincide with those of 1794–5). He has, however, chosen to date the story back to the American War which had ended in 1783. To judge from l. 133, the Pedlar and Poet should be thought of as meeting sometime in the mid 1780s.

143–4 Compare Job, 7.10, 'He shall return no more to his house, *neither shall his place know him any more*', and Psalms, 103. 15–16:

As for man, his days are as grass: as a flower
of the field, so he flourisheth.

To numerous self-denials, Margaret
Went struggling on through those calamitous years
With chearful hope. But ere the second autumn,
A fever seized her husband. In disease
He lingered long, and when his strength returned   150
He found the little he had stored to meet
The hour of accident, or crippling age,
Was all consumed. As I have said, 'twas now
A time of trouble: shoals of artisans
Were from their daily labour turned away   155
To hang for bread on parish charity,
They and their wives and children – happier far
Could they have lived as do the little birds
That peck along the hedges, or the kite
That makes her dwelling in the mountain rocks.   160
      Ill fared it now with Robert, he who dwelt
In this poor cottage. At his door he stood
And whistled many a snatch of merry tunes
That had no mirth in them, or with his knife
Carved uncouth figures on the heads of sticks;   165
Then idly sought about through every nook
Of house or garden any casual task
Of use or ornament, and with a strange
Amusing but uneasy novelty
He blended where he might the various tasks   170
Of summer, autumn, winter, and of spring.
But this endured not, his good humour soon
Became a weight in which no pleasure was,
And poverty brought on a petted mood
And a sore temper. Day by day he drooped,   175
And he would leave his home, and to the town
Without an errand would he turn his steps,
Or wander here and there among the fields.
One while he would speak lightly of his babes

        For the wind passeth over it, and it is gone;
        and the place thereof shall know it no more.
    For the appalling social conditions at the time when Wordsworth was
writing, see Eden's *State of the Poor* (1797) and Malthus' famous *Essay on
the Principles of Population* (1798).
154   **shoals** crowds. **artisans** workmen.
156   **parish charity** parishes were bound by law to support their own poor,
but given no central funds with which to do so.

And with a cruel tongue; at other times
He played with them wild freaks of merriment,
And 'twas a piteous thing to see the looks
Of the poor innocent children. "Every smile",
Said Margaret to me here beneath these trees,
"Made my heart bleed." '
                              At this the old man paused,
And looking up to those enormous elms
He said, ' 'Tis now the hour of deepest noon.
At this still season of repose and peace,
This hour when all things which are not at rest
Are chearful, while this multitude of flies
Fills all the air with happy melody,
Why should a tear be in an old man's eye?
Why should we thus with an untoward mind,
And in the weakness of humanity,
From natural wisdom turn our hearts away,
To natural comfort shut our eyes and ears,
And feeding on disquiet, thus disturb
The calm of Nature with our restless thoughts?'

Second Part

He spake with somewhat of a solemn tone,
But when he ended there was in his face
Such easy chearfulness, a look so mild,
That for a little time it stole away
All recollection, and that simple tale
Passed from my mind like a forgotten sound.
A while on trivial things we held discourse,
To me soon tasteless. In my own despite
I thought of that poor woman as of one
Whom I had known and loved. He had rehearsed
Her homely tale with such familiar power,
With such an active countenance, an eye
So busy, that the things of which he spake
Seemed present, and, attention now relaxed,
There was a heartfelt chillness in my veins.
I rose, and turning from that breezy shade

206   **tasteless**   insipid.

Went out into the open air, and stood   215
To drink the comfort of the warmer sun.
Long time I had not stayed ere, looking round
Upon that tranquil ruin, I returned
And begged of the old man that for my sake
He would resume his story.
                              He replied,   220
'It were a wantonness, and would demand
Severe reproof, if we were men whose hearts
Could hold vain dalliance with the misery
Even of the dead, contented thence to draw
A momentary pleasure, never marked   225
By reason, barren of all future good.
But we have known that there is often found
In mournful thoughts, and always might be found,
A power to virtue friendly; were't not so
I am a dreamer among men, indeed   230
An idle dreamer. 'Tis a common tale
By moving accidents uncharactered,
A tale of silent suffering, hardly clothed
In bodily form, and to the grosser sense
But ill adapted – scarcely palpable   235
To him who does not think. But at your bidding
I will proceed.
                  While thus it fared with them
To whom this cottage till that hapless year
Had been a blessed home, it was my chance
To travel in a country far remote;   240
And glad I was when, halting by yon gate
That leads from the green lane, again I saw
These lofty elm-trees. Long I did not rest –
With many pleasant thoughts I cheered my way
O'er the flat common. At the door arrived,   245

---

221   **wantonness** self-indulgence.
231–6 See Introduction, above, pp. 1–2, for Wordsworth's strong views about
       poetry that is marked ('characterized') by exciting events ('moving acci-
       dents'). In the Preface to *Lyrical Ballads* he refers to his contemporaries'
       'degrading thirst after outrageous stimulation'; his priggishness no
       doubt reflects a fear that readers would prefer sensationalism to his own
       'tales of silent suffering'.
235   **palpable** perceptible – the unthinking would scarcely notice there *was*
       a story.

I knocked, and when I entered, with the hope
Of usual greeting, Margaret looked at me
A little while, then turned her head away
Speechless, and sitting down upon a chair
Wept bitterly. I wist not what to do,
Or how to speak to her. Poor wretch, at last
She rose from off her seat, and then, oh sir,
I cannot tell how she pronounced my name.
With fervent love, and with a face of grief
Unutterably helpless, and a look
That seemed to cling upon me, she enquired
If I had seen her husband. As she spake
A strange surprise and fear came to my heart,
Nor had I power to answer ere she told
That he had disappeared – just two months gone
He left his house: two wretched days had passed,
And on the third by the first break of light,
Within her casement full in view she saw
A purse of gold. "I trembled at the sight",
Said Margaret, "for I knew it was his hand
That placed it there. And on that very day
By one, a stranger, from my husband sent,
The tidings came that he had joined a troop
Of soldiers going to a distant land.
He left me thus. Poor man, he had not heart
To take a farewell of me, and he feared
That I should follow with my babes, and sink
Beneath the misery of a soldier's life."
       This tale did Margaret tell with many tears,
And when she ended I had little power
To give her comfort, and was glad to take

---

250   **wist** knew.
264   **A purse of gold** the 'bounty' of three guineas paid to men when they
       enlisted. Men with starving families were not in a position to refuse. In
       1797, when Wordsworth was writing, the price of a four-pound loaf was
       sevenpence halfpenny (a guinea was 21 shillings, or 105 new pence). In
       1800 the price more than doubled, largely as a result of the War.
269   **a distant land** presumably America (see ll. 133–8n, above).
270–3 In Wordsworth's *Female Vagrant* (published in *Lyrical Ballads*, 1798, but
       probably written in 1791) the central character is a woman who does fol-
       low her husband when he enlists. She herself survives, and is sent home
       to a life of begging; her husband and three children die. It must have
       been a very common story.

Such words of hope from her own mouth as served
To cheer us both. But long we had not talked
Ere we built up a pile of better thoughts,   *like a horse*
And with a brighter eye she looked around   280
As if she had been shedding tears of joy.
We parted. It was then the early spring;
I left her busy with her garden tools,
And well remember, o'er that fence she looked,
And, while I paced along the foot-way path,   285
Called out and sent a blessing after me,
With tender chearfulness, and with a voice
That seemed the very sound of happy thoughts.
    I roved o'er many a hill and many a dale
With this my weary load, in heat and cold,   290
Through many a wood and many an open ground,
In sunshine or in shade, in wet or fair,
Now blithe, now drooping, as it might befal;
My best companions now the driving winds
And now the "trotting brooks" and whispering trees,   295
And now the music of my own sad steps,
With many a short-lived thought that passed between
And disappeared.
              I came this way again
Towards the wane of summer, when the wheat
Was yellow, and the soft and bladed grass   300
Sprang up afresh and o'er the hayfield spread
Its tender green. When I had reached the door
I found that she was absent. In the shade,
Where we now sit, I waited her return.
Her cottage in its outward look appeared   305
As chearful as before, in any shew
Of neatness little changed – but that I thought

295   Wordsworth uses inverted commas to draw attention to a passage in
      Burns' *Epistle to William Simpson*, which is about the poet and his relation-
      ship to Nature. Burns was important to him at this period because he
      too had written about ordinary country people, and MS.B of *The Ruined
      Cottage* (March 1798) has as its epigraph appropriate lines from the
      Epistle to J. Lapraik:
                Give me a spark of Nature's fire
                'Tis the best learning I desire . . .
                My Muse though homely in attire
                May touch the heart.

The honeysuckle crowded round the door
And from the wall hung down in heavier tufts,
And knots of worthless stonecrop started out
Along the window's edge, and grew like weeds
Against the lower panes. I turned aside
And strolled into her garden. It was changed.
The unprofitable bindweed spread his bells
From side to side, and with unwieldy wreaths
Had dragged the rose from its sustaining wall
And bent it down to earth. The border tufts,
Daisy, and thrift, and lowly camomile,
And thyme, had straggled out into the paths
Which they were used to deck.
                               Ere this an hour
Was wasted. Back I turned my restless steps,
And as I walked before the door it chanced
A stranger passed, and guessing whom I sought,
He said that she was used to ramble far.
The sun was sinking in the west, and now
I sate with sad impatience. From within
Her solitary infant cried aloud.
The spot though fair seemed very desolate –
The longer I remained more desolate –
And looking round I saw the corner-stones,
Till then unmarked, on either side the door

314–20   For the symbolic implications of Margaret's garden, see Introduc-
         tion, pp. 9–12 above. In the background is the Swiss peasant's cottage
         of *Descriptive Studies* (1792), naively typifying industry and happiness:
               The casement shade more luscious woodbine binds,
               And to the door a neater pathway winds . . .
                              (ll. 726–7 and ff)
         The 'unprofitable' bindweed and 'straggling' herbs probably show a
         further recollection of Goldsmith:
               Beside yon straggling fence that skirts the way,
               With blossomed furze unprofitably gay
                         (*Deserted Village*, 193–4)
330–6   Wordsworth is incorporating an observation from Dorothy's *Journal*
         about 'sheep, that leave locks of wool, and the red marks with which
         they are spotted' on wooden palings by the road. The entry belongs to
         4 February 1798, and is a reminder that although the central section of
         The Ruined Cottage (ll. 237–443, including the Pedlar's four visits to
         Margaret) seems to have been written in summer 1797, it was no doubt
         revised and extended the following spring.

With dull red stains discoloured, and stuck o'er
With tufts and hairs of wool, as if the sheep
That feed upon the commons thither came
Familiarly, and found a couching-place   335
Even at her threshold.
                The house-clock struck eight:
I turned and saw her distant a few steps.
Her face was pale and thin, her figure too
Was changed. As she unlocked the door she said,
"It grieves me you have waited here so long,   340
But in good truth I've wandered much of late,
And sometimes – to my shame I speak – have need
Of my best prayers to bring me back again."
While on the board she spread our evening meal
She told me she had lost her elder child,   345
That he for months had been a serving-boy,
Apprenticed by the parish. "I perceive
You look at me, and you have cause. Today
I have been travelling far, and many days
About the fields I wander, knowing this   350
Only, that what I seek I cannot find.
And so I waste my time: for I am changed,
And to myself", said she, "have done much wrong,
And to this helpless infant. I have slept
Weeping, and weeping I have waked. My tears   355
Have flowed as if my body were not such
As others are, and I could never die.
But I am now in mind and in my heart
More easy, and I hope", said she, "that heaven
Will give me patience to endure the things   360
Which I behold at home."
                It would have grieved

339–54   It is not entirely clear what sort of wrong Margaret thinks she has
done to herself and her child, but ll. 341–3 suggest she has been tempted
by suicide, which was condemned by the Church as a sin (see *Brothers*,
389). It is interesting that a number of very strong echoes connect her
wandering, and the Pedlar's waiting (ll. 321–37), to Wordsworth's study
in *The Borderers* (ii.i. 14–31) of a woman driven by grief to actual insanity.
In *The Ruined Cottage* we are offered obsessional behaviour – the compul-
sive seeking for Robert – but it is well understood by Margaret herself,
and never even verges on madness.

344   **board**   table.

Your very soul to see her. Sir, I feel
The story linger in my heart. I fear
'Tis long and tedious, but my spirit clings
To that poor woman. So familiarly   3
Do I perceive her manner and her look
And presence, and so deeply do I feel
Her goodness, that not seldom in my walks
A momentary trance comes over me
And to myself I seem to muse on one   3
By sorrow laid asleep or borne away,
A human being destined to awake
To human life, or something very near
To human life, when he shall come again
For whom she suffered. Sir, it would have grieved   3
Your very soul to see her: evermore
Her eyelids drooped, her eyes were downward cast,
And when she at her table gave me food
She did not look at me. Her voice was low,
Her body was subdued. In every act   3
Pertaining to her house-affairs appeared
The careless stillness which a thinking mind
Gives to an idle matter. Still she sighed,
But yet no motion of the breast was seen,
No heaving of the heart. While by the fire   3
We sate together, sighs came on my ear –
I knew not how, and hardly whence, they came.
I took my staff, and when I kissed her babe
The tears stood in her eyes. I left her then
With the best hope and comfort I could give: 3
She thanked me for my will, but for my hope
It seemed she did not thank me.
                                      I returned
And took my rounds along this road again
Ere on its sunny bank the primrose flower
Had chronicled the earliest day of spring.   3
I found her sad and drooping. She had learned

379–83   Compare *Old Man Travelling*, 4–8, written in May–June 1797:
                                      every limb,
          His look and bending figure, all bespeak
          A man who does not move with pain, but moves
          With thought. He is insensibly subdued
          To settled quiet . . .

No tidings of her husband. If he lived,
She knew not that he lived: if he were dead,
She knew not he was dead. She seemed the same
In person or appearance, but her house   400
Bespoke a sleepy hand of negligence.
The floor was neither dry nor neat, the hearth
Was comfortless,
The windows too were dim, and her few books,
Which one upon the other heretofore   405
Had been piled up against the corner-panes
In seemly order, now with straggling leaves
Lay scattered here and there, open or shut,
As they had chanced to fall. Her infant babe
Had from its mother caught the trick of grief, 410
And sighed among its playthings. Once again
I turned towards the garden-gate, and saw
More plainly still that poverty and grief
Were now come nearer to her. The earth was hard,
With weeds defaced and knots of withered grass; 415
No ridges there appeared of clear black mould,
No winter greenness. Of her herbs and flowers
It seemed the better part were gnawed away
Or trampled on the earth. A chain of straw,
Which had been twisted round the tender stem   420
Of a young appletree, lay at its root;
The bark was nibbled round by truant sheep.
Margaret stood near, her infant in her arms,
And, seeing that my eye was on the tree,
She said, "I fear it will be dead and gone   425
Ere Robert come again."
                          Towards the house
Together we returned, and she inquired
If I had any hope. But for her babe,
And for her little friendless boy, she said,
She had no wish to live – that she must die   430
Of sorrow. Yet I saw the idle loom

---

403   Line defective in the manuscript.
404   **her few books**   though of a lower social class than the Ewbanks (*The Brothers*) and Michael, who own inherited land, Margaret apparently knows how to read. See *Michael*, 444n.
410   **trick**   habit.

Still in its place. His Sunday garments hung
Upon the self-same nail, his very staff
Stood undisturbed behind the door. And when
I passed this way beaten by autumn winds,
She told me that her little babe was dead
And she was left alone. That very time,
I yet remember, through the miry lane
She walked with me a mile, when the bare trees
Trickled with foggy damps, and in such sort
That any heart had ached to hear her, begged
That wheresoe'er I went I still would ask
For him whom she had lost. We parted then,
Our final parting; for from that time forth
Did many seasons pass ere I returned
Into this tract again.
                    Five tedious years
She lingered in unquiet widowhood,
A wife and widow. Needs must it have been
A sore heart-wasting. I have heard, my friend,
That in that broken arbour she would sit
The idle length of half a sabbath day –
There, where you see the toadstool's lazy head –
And when a dog passed by she still would quit
The shade and look abroad. On this old bench
For hours she sate, and evermore her eye
Was busy in the distance, shaping things
Which made her heart beat quick. Seest thou that path? –
The green-sward now has broken its grey line –
There to and fro she paced through many a day

446   **tract**   region, district. For no obvious reason, Margaret survives not
      'Five tedious years' but nine, in *The Excursion* (and 'ten years gone' in
      l. 133 becomes 'not twenty years ago').
455–92   Wordsworth stated in his Fenwick Note of 1843 that ll. 446–92,
      describing Margaret's last years and death were the first part of *The
      Ruined Cottage* to be written. Evidence that he did indeed begin at the end
      is to be found in Dorothy's transcription of ll. 455–92 for Coleridge on
      10 June 1797, and in the fact that these lines – beginning 'her eye / Was
      busy in the distance' – have a specific literary source: Southey's account
      of a war-widow in *Joan of Arc*, Book VII (quoted, together with Dorothy's
      transcription, Introduction, pp. 3–5 above).
459–62   Robert had been a weaver, and Margaret supports herself in her last
      years by spinning flax. Compare the situation in *Brothers*, 20–5, and
      Michael, 84–7 (and note).

Of the warm summer, from a belt of flax   460
That girt her waist, spinning the long-drawn thread
With backward steps. Yet ever as there passed
A man whose garments shewed the soldier's red,
Or crippled mendicant in sailor's garb,
The little child who sate to turn the wheel   465
Ceased from his toil, and she, with faltering voice,
Expecting still to learn her husband's fate,
Made many a fond inquiry; and when they
Whose presence gave no comfort were gone by,
Her heart was still more sad. And by yon gate,   470
Which bars the traveller's road, she often stood,
And when a stranger horseman came, the latch
Would lift, and in his face look wistfully,
Most happy if from aught discovered there
Of tender feeling she might dare repeat   475
The same sad question.
                Meanwhile her poor hut
Sunk to decay; for he was gone, whose hand
At the first nippings of October frost
Closed up each chink, and with fresh bands of straw
Chequered the green-grown thatch. And so she lived   480
Through the long winter, reckless and alone,
Till this reft house, by frost, and thaw, and rain,
Was sapped; and when she slept, the nightly damps
Did chill her breast, and in the stormy day
Her tattered clothes were ruffled by the wind   485
Even at the side of her own fire. Yet still
She loved this wretched spot, nor would for worlds
Have parted hence; and still that length of road,

462–8   The British army wore red until the end of the nineteenth century.
464   **mendicant**   beggar.
467   **still**   always.
468   **fond**   tender; but also, foolish.
480–90   Compare the widow's situation in Southey's *Joan of Arc*, which seems
      to have been Wordsworth's starting-point:
                  Nor ever shall she know
          Her husband dead, but *tortured with vain hope*,
          Gaze on . . .
      (See Introduction, above, pp. 4–5.)
481   **reckless**   uncaring, desperate.
482   **reft**   bereft – i.e. without Robert.

And this rude bench, one torturing hope endeared,
Fast rooted at her heart. And here, my friend,
In sickness she remained; and here she died,
Last human tenant of these ruined walls.'
    The old man ceased; he saw that I was moved.
From that low Bench rising instinctively
I turned aside in weakness, nor had power
To thank him for the tale which he had told.
I stood, and leaning o'er the garden gate

492   **Last human tenant**   the cottage is now tenanted (occupied) by animals – 'The unshod colt, / The wandering heifer, and the potter's ass', of ll. 111–12. *The Ruined Cottage* originally ended at this point; all that follows belongs to spring 1798.

493–500   The response of the listening Poet to Margaret's story is of great importance to Wordsworth as a way of suggesting how the reader himself might respond. It enabled him to show poetry as having the moral influence which he and Coleridge believed it could exert on a wider audience if given the chance. The Poet's blessing of Margaret 'in the impotence of grief' recalls *The Ancient Mariner*, where the redemptive act of blessing the water-snakes is similarly instinctive – 'And I blessed them *unawares*' (l. 279). Wordsworth's phrase, '*it* seemed / to comfort me', can refer either to the Poet's reviewing Margaret's sufferings, or to the gate on which he is leaning (compare his Fenwick Note to *Intimations*: 'Many times while going to school have I grasped at a wall or tree to recall myself from this abyss of idealism to reality').

497–506   Wordsworth made a number of drafts before arriving at his final account of the Poet's response to Margaret's story. The first is of especial interest, both in its own right, and for a further link with *The Ancient Mariner*:

> And when at last brought back from my own mind
> I looked around, the cottage and the elms,
> The road, the pathway, and the garden wall
> Which old, and loose, and mossy, o'er the road
> Hung bellying, all appeared – I know not how,
> But to some eye within me all appeared –
> Colours and forms of a strange discipline.
> The trouble which they sent into my thought
> Was sweet; I looked, and looked again, *and to myself*
> *I seemed a better and a wiser man.*
>   (*Butler*, 256–7)

Compare the final lines of Coleridge's poem,

> A sadder and a wiser man
> He rose the morrow morn.

On this occasion Wordsworth could well be the earlier of the two: the *Ruined Cottage* draft was written certainly before 10 March 1798, and *The Ancient Mariner* completed (in its full-length version) on the 23rd.

Reviewed that woman's sufferings; and it seemed
To comfort me while with a brother's love
I blessed her in the impotence of grief.   500
At length towards the cottage I returned
Fondly, and traced with milder interest
That secret spirit of humanity
Which, mid the calm oblivious tendencies
Of Nature, mid her plants, her weeds and flowers,   505
And silent overgrowings, still survived.
The old man seeing this resumed, and said,
'My friend, enough to sorrow have you given,
The purposes of wisdom ask no more:
Be wise and chearful, and no longer read   510
The forms of things with an unworthy eye:
She sleeps in the calm earth, and peace is here.
I well remember that those very plumes,
Those weeds, and the high speargrass on that wall,
By mist and silent raindrops silvered o'er,   515
As once I passed did to my mind convey
So still an image of tranquility,
So calm and still, and looked so beautiful
Amid the uneasy thoughts which filled my mind,
That what we feel of sorrow and despair   520
From ruin and from change, and all the grief
The passing shews of being leave behind,
Appeared an idle dream that could not live
Where meditation was. I turned away,

504   **oblivious tendencies**   Nature is both oblivious herself, in the sense of
      'unmindful', 'unconcerned', and has the tendency to cause forgetful-
      ness in others by quietly obliterating traces of human life.
510–11   That is, do not be misled by the outward appearances. The Pedlar
      himself had

                            an eye which evermore
            Looked deep into the shades of difference
            As they lie hid in all exterior forms . . .
                        (*Pedlar*, 346–8)

520–4   After the poem has placed such value on human emotion it seems
      extraordinary that we should be asked to think of Margaret's life as a
      'passing shew of being', and to regard our own feelings of sorrow and
      despair as merely 'an idle dream'. Behind the apparent harshness, how-
      ever, lies the philosophy of Bishop Berkeley (1685–1753), who was the
      major influence on Coleridge at this period, and a source of his confi-
      dence in the future of mankind. Wordsworth had especially in mind

Constantly reminding us of retrospecting and constitedness of
story by Pedlar's repeated return to hear what has happened in
the interval.

And walked along my road in happiness.'
	He ceased. By this the sun declining shot
A slant and mellow radiance, which began
To fall upon us where beneath the trees
We sate on that low bench. And now we felt,
Admonished thus, the sweet hour coming on:
A linnet warbled from those lofty elms,
A thrush sang loud, and other melodies
At distance heard peopled the milder air.
The old man rose and hoisted up his load;
Together casting then a farewell look
Upon those silent walls, we left the shade,
And ere the stars were visible attained
A rustic inn, our evening resting-place.

ll. 413–19 of *Religious Musings*, which Coleridge in 1797 footnoted as drawing on Berkeley:

> Believe thou, O my soul,
>   Life is a vision shadowy of Truth,
>   And vice, and anguish, and the wormy grave,
>   Shapes of a dream. The veiling clouds retire,
>   And lo! – the throne of the redeeming God . . .

Unlike Coleridge (and many others at this period), Wordsworth did not expect a Christian apocalypse, but the Pedlar's meditation does nevertheless ask us to see Margaret's life, and death, in terms of universal harmony.

526–34   The presence of *Lycidas* is felt throughout Wordsworth's final paragraph. As the old Pedlar rises and hoists his pack onto his shoulders the recollection of Milton's famous concluding lines is a little incongruous:

> At last he rose, and twitched his mantle blue:
> Tomorrow to fresh woods and pastures new.

The Brothers

'These tourists, heaven preserve us, needs must live
A profitable life! Some glance along,
Rapid and gay, as if the earth were air,
And they were butterflies to wheel about
Long as their summer lasted; some – as wise –   5
Upon the forehead of a jutting crag
Sit perched with book and pencil on their knee,
And look and scribble, scribble on and look,
Until a man might travel twelve stout miles
Or reap an acre of his neighbour's corn.   10
    But, for that moping son of idleness –

---

1   *The Brothers* is based on a story that Wordsworth and Coleridge heard on
     a walking-tour of the Lake District in 1799 (see Introduction above). It
     was probably to some extent planned on the walk, and by Christmas
     Eve – only four days after Wordsworth and Dorothy arrived to live at
     Dove Cottage – the poet was complaining to Coleridge: 'I am afraid it
     will have one fault, that of being too long' (*EY*, 237). *Hart-Leap Well* we
     know was written in the middle of work on *The Brothers*, but the poem was
     almost certainly completed before Wordsworth started on *Home at
     Grasmere* at the beginning of March 1800. There is manuscript evidence
     to suggest that the first lines to be written were those describing the
     death of James Ewbank. As in the case of *The Ruined Cottage*, Wordsworth
     seems to have gone back at a secondary stage to create the main part of
     his story.
         Notes printed below in italics are from the first edition of the poem
     in *Lyrical Ballads* 1800.

1–10 *This poem was intended to be the concluding poem of a series of pastorals, the scene
     of which was laid among the mountains of Cumberland and Westmoreland. I
     mention this to apologise for the abruptness with which the poem begins. W.W.*

     Wordsworth nowhere else mentions this scheme; but he does in
     several other cases (*The Thorn* and *Norman Boy*, for instance) show anxiety
     at this period about the abruptness with which poems open. Four
     poems in *Lyrical Ballads*, volume two, are subtitled 'pastorals' (*The Oak
     and The Broom*, *The Idle Shepherd-Boys*, *The Pet Lamb* and *Michael*), but only
     Michael is similar to *The Brothers* in scope and intention. For
     Wordsworth's important letters of 1801 connecting the two poems, see
     Introduction, pp. 19–20 above.

11–12 Wordsworth seems to be recalling the 'wealthy son of commerce' who

47

Why can he tarry *yonder*? In our churchyard
Is neither epitaph nor monument,
Tomb-stone nor name, only the turf we tread
And a few natural graves.' To Jane, his wife,
Thus spake the homely priest of Ennerdale.
It was a July evening, and he sate
Upon the long stone-seat beneath the eaves
Of his old cottage – as it chanced that day,
Employed in winter's work. Upon the stone
His wife sate near him, teasing matted wool,
While from the twin cards toothed with glittering wire,
He fed the spindle of his youngest child,
Who turned her large round wheel in the open air
With back and forward steps. Towards the field
In which the parish chapel stood alone
Girt round with a bare ring of mossy wall,
While half an hour went by, the priest had sent
Many a long look of wonder; and at last,
Risen from his seat, beside the snow-white ridge
Of carded wool which the old man had piled
He laid his implements with gentle care,
Each in the other locked, and down the path
Which from his cottage to the churchyard led
He took his way, impatient to accost
The stranger whom he saw still lingering there.
    'Twas one well known to him in former days:
A shepherd-lad, who ere his thirteenth year

had sauntered by at the beginning of Coleridge's early poem, *Lines Written Upon Leaving a Place of Retirement* (1796).

15–16 Ennerdale is still a very remote valley, but the Priest's opening words – ' "These tourists, heaven preserve us!" ' – are a reminder that more and more visitors had been coming to the Lake District during the twenty years before Wordsworth was writing. Guidebooks, such as Thomas West's, 1785 (which included Gray's *Journal of a Visit to the Lakes* in later editions), and picturesque 'Tours' (such as William Gilpin's, 1786), instructed readers in what they should expect, and how they should respond.

20–4 Wordsworth has in mind Margaret 'spinning the long-drawn thread / With backward steps' (*Ruined Cottage*, 459–62). Lines 27–8 also contain *Ruined Cottage* echoes, and it is especially clear at this point that he is modelling himself on the earlier poem.

22 **twin cards** a pair of combs used for teasing out the hairs of wool before they are spun into a thread.

Had changed his calling – with the mariners
A fellow-mariner – and so had fared   40
Through twenty seasons; but he had been reared
Among the mountains, and he in his heart
Was half a shepherd on the stormy seas.
Oft in the piping shrouds had Leonard heard
The tones of waterfalls, and inland sounds   45
Of caves and trees. And when the regular wind
Between the tropics filled the steady sail
And blew with the same breath through days and weeks,
Lengthening invisibly its weary line
Along the cloudless main, he, in those hours   50
Of tiresome indolence, would often hang
Over the vessel's side and gaze and gaze;
And while the broad green wave and sparkling foam
Flashed round him images and hues that wrought
In union with the employment of his heart,   55
He – thus by feverish passion overcome –
Even with the organs of his bodily eye,
Below him in the bosom of the deep
Saw mountains, saw the forms of sheep that grazed
On verdant hills, with dwellings among trees,   60

39–40   Leonard has not merely become a sailor, but entered into a new fel-
lowship, joined a new community with its own special bonds. Note the
distinction, however, between 'fellow-mariners' and '*brother* shepherds'
(l. 72), '*brother* fountains' (l. 141).

44   **shrouds**   fixed ropes that support the mast of a ship and are frequently
climbed when changing sail. The wind would no doubt 'pipe' through
them.

54–5   **wrought . . . heart**   the green waves help Leonard in recreating the
landscapes that his heart is yearning for.

56–62   *This description of the calenture is sketched from an imperfect recollection of an
admirable one in prose, by Mr. Gilbert, author of 'The Hurricane'.* W.W.

While believing that the poet's creativity should never be subjected
to 'the chains of circumstance and mere fact', Wordsworth quite often
claimed that his work had a scientific basis (*Goody Blake and Harry Gill*, for
instance, is said to be founded on 'a well-authenticated fact'). Leonard
does not of course actually suffer from the calenture (defined in
Johnson's *Dictionary* as 'a distemper peculiar to sailors in hot climates;
wherein they imagine the sea to be green fields, and will throw them-
selves into it'), but has a comparable imaginative experience brought
on by the strength of his love.

And shepherds clad in the same country grey
Which he himself had worn.
                                        And now at length,
From perils manifold, with some small wealth
Acquired by traffic in the Indian Isles,
To his paternal home he is returned
With a determined purpose to resume
The life which he lived there – both for the sake
Of many darling pleasures, and the love
Which to an only brother he has borne
In all his hardships, since that happy time
When, whether it blew foul or fair, they two
Were brother shepherds on their native hills.
They were the last of all their race; and now,
When Leonard had approached his home, his heart
Failed in him, and not venturing to inquire
Tidings of one whom he so dearly loved,
Towards the churchyard he had turned aside
That (as he knew in what particular spot
His family were laid) he thence might learn
If still his brother lived, or to the file
Another grave was added. He had found
Another grave, near which a full half-hour
He had remained; but as he gazed there grew
Such a confusion in his memory
That he began to doubt, and he had hopes
That he had seen this heap of turf before –

61   **country grey**   clothes woven from undyed wool of the local Herdwick
       sheep.
64   **traffic in the Indian Isles**   trade in the East Indies.
73–81   Wordsworth is basing the character of Leonard on that of his own
       brother, John, who was also a sailor (soon to be appointed Commander
       of the East Indiaman, *Earl of Abergavenny*), and also hoping to make
       enough money from trade to return and live permanently in the Lake
       District. The detail of Leonard's not daring to ask for news (ll. 74–6)
       seems to have been suggested by John's behaviour when he arrived at
       Dove Cottage at the end of January 1800, actually while *The Brothers* was
       being written. After twice not being able to bring himself to knock at the
       door, he had to go to the local inn and send a message to the poet and
       Dorothy (*EY*, 649). For Wordsworth's closeness to John, and the bonds
       between them, see *EY*, 547–9, 559–61, written after John was drowned at
       sea in February 1805.
80   **file**   row, line.

That it was not another grave, but one
He had forgotten. He had lost his path
As up the vale he came that afternoon
Through fields which once had been well known to him,   90
And oh, what joy the recollection now
Sent to his heart! He lifted up his eyes,
And looking round he thought that he perceived
Strange alteration wrought on every side
Among the woods and fields, and that the rocks,   95
And the eternal hills themselves, were changed.
     By this the priest, who down the field had come
Unseen by Leonard, at the churchyard gate
Stopped short; and thence, at leisure, limb by limb
He scanned him with a gay complacency.   100
'Aye', thought the vicar, smiling to himself,
' 'Tis one of those who needs must leave the path
Of the world's business, to go wild alone –
His arms have a perpetual holiday.
The happy man will creep about the fields   105
Following his fancies by the hour, to bring
Tears down his cheek, or solitary smiles
Into his face, until the setting sun
Write Fool upon his forehead.' Planted thus
Beneath a shed that overarched the gate   110
Of this rude churchyard, till the stars appeared
The good man might have communed with himself,
But that the stranger, who had left the grave,
Approached. He recognized the priest at once,
And after greetings interchanged (and given   115
By Leonard to the vicar as to one
Unknown to him), this dialogue ensued.

99–100 Wordsworth is echoing Shakespeare, *Troilus and Cressida*, IV. v. 238–9:
               I will the second time,
     As I would buy thee, view thee limb by limb . . .
100   **complacency** still at this period has the neutral meaning of
    'pleasure', but the modern sense of 'smugness' would be quite appro-
    priate to the Priest's behaviour.
108–9 Unlike the Pedlar of *The Ruined Cottage*, the Priest is to some extent
    characterized through style. Here his self-importance is conveyed in the
    imitation of Shakespearean metaphor. Compare *Richard II*, III. ii. 147–
    8:
              And with rainy eyes
     Write sorrow on the bosom of the earth.

LEONARD

You live, sir, in these dales, a quiet life.
Your years make up one peaceful family,
And who would grieve and fret, if – welcome come   12
And welcome gone – they are so like each other
They cannot be remembered? Scarce a funeral
Comes to this churchyard once in eighteen months;
And yet, some changes must take place among you.
And you who dwell here, even among these rocks   12
Can trace the finger of mortality,
And see that with our threescore years and ten
We are not all that perish. I remember
(For many years ago I passed this road)
There was a footway all along the fields   13
By the brook-side; 'tis gone. And that dark cleft –
To me it does not seem to wear the face
Which then it had.

PRIEST

Why, sir, for aught I know,
That chasm is much the same.

LEONARD

But surely, yonder –

PRIEST

Aye, there indeed your memory is a friend   13
That does not play you false. On that tall pike
(It is the loneliest place of all these hills)
There were two springs which bubbled side by side
As if they had been made that they might be

---

126   **the finger of mortality**   signs of death or change.

137–43   *The impressive circumstances here described actually took place some years ago in*
this country, upon an eminence called Kidstow Pike, one of the highest of the moun-
tains that surround Hawes Water. The summit of the pike was stricken by lightning,
and every trace of one of the fountains disappeared, while the other continued to flow
as before. W.W.

As with his note on the calenture (ll. 56–62), Wordsworth wishes us
to know that his description has a basis in fact. He takes it for granted
that we shall also notice its symbolic implication, and think of the two
'fountains' (springs) in terms of Leonard and James; see Introduction
pp. 15–16, above.

Companions for each other! Ten years back,   140
Close to those brother fountains, the huge crag
Was rent with lightning – one is dead and gone,
The other, left behind, is flowing still.
For accidents and changes such as these,
Why, we have store of them! A water-spout   145
Will bring down half a mountain – what a feast
For folks that wander up and down like you,
To see an acre's breadth of that wide cliff
One roaring cataract! A sharp May storm
Will come with loads of January snow   150
And in one night send twenty score of sheep
To feed the ravens; or a shepherd dies
By some untoward death among the rocks;
The ice breaks up, and sweeps away a bridge;
A wood is felled. And then, for our own homes –   155
A child is born or christened, a field ploughed,
A daughter sent to service, a web spun,
The old house-clock is decked with a new face –
And hence, so far from wanting facts or dates
To chronicle the time, we all have here   160
A pair of diaries: one serving, sir,
For the whole dale, and one for each fireside.
Yours was a stranger's judgment – for historians
Commend me to these vallies!

LEONARD
                Yet your churchyard
Seems (if such freedom may be used with you)   165

145   **store** plenty.

151–2   The raven, largest and most impressive member of the crow family, is still quite common in the Lake District. Like other crows it is a scavenger.

153–4   What will later be seen as a reference to James' death is slipped (at l. 144) into a list of local 'accidents', happenings, occurrences.

157   **sent to service** sent to become a maidservant in one of the more prosperous local families. The practice, which came to an end with the 1939 War, was not felt in any way to be degrading.
        a web spun a piece of cloth is woven.

161–4   Time in the vale is measured by memory of important, and not-so-important, events. Some are general, and recorded in the 'diary' that is the outer world; others are private, and found in the 'diary' of the fireside, or family.

To say that you are heedless of the past.
Here's neither head nor foot-stone, plate or brass –
An orphan could not find his mother's grave –
Cross-bones or skull, type of our earthly state
Or emblem of our hopes. The dead man's home   1
Is but a fellow to that pasture field.

PRIEST

Why there, sir, is a thought that's new to me.
The stone-cutters, 'tis true, might beg their bread
If every English churchyard were like ours;
Yet your conclusion wanders from the truth.   1
We have no need of names and epitaphs,
We talk about the dead by our firesides.
And then for our immortal part – *we* want
No symbols, sir, to tell us that plain tale.
The thought of death sits easy on the man   1
Who has been born and dies among the mountains.

LEONARD

Your dalesmen, then, do in each other's thoughts
Possess a kind of second life. No doubt
You, sir, could help me to the history
Of half these graves?

PRIEST

                    For eight-score winters past –   1
With what I've witnessed, and with what I've heard –
Perhaps I might; and on a winter's evening,
If you were seated at my chimney's nook,

167–70   The skull is a 'type' (symbol) of our earthly state (mortality); and the
         bones, in the form of a cross, are an emblem of hopes for an after-life
         that depend on the Crucifixion. Carvings of the skull and crossed bones
         on tombs appear first in the period that followed the Black Death in
         1350.
176–81   *There is not anything more worthy of remark in the manners of the inhabitants of
         these mountains, than the tranquility, I might say indifference, with which they think
         and talk about the subject of death. Some of the country churchyards, as here
         described, do not contain a single tombstone, and most of them have a very small
         number.* W.W.

By turning o'er these hillocks one by one
We two could travel, sir, through a strange round,   190
Yet all in the broad highway of the world.
Now there's a grave – your foot is half upon it –
It looks just like the rest, and yet that man
Died broken-hearted.

LEONARD

'Tis a common cause –
We'll take another. Who is he that lies   195
Beneath yon ridge, the last of those three graves? –
It touches on that piece of native rock
Left in the churchyard wall.

PRIEST

That's Walter Ewbank.
He had as white a head and fresh a cheek
As ever were produced by youth and age   200
Engendering in the blood of hale fourscore.
For five long generations had the heart
Of Walter's forefathers o'erflowed the bounds
Of their inheritance – that single cottage
(You see it yonder), and those few green fields.   205
They toiled and wrought, and still, from sire to son,
Each struggled, and each yielded as before
A little – yet a little. And old Walter –

189–91 By mentally opening the graves – going over in turn the stories of
their occupants – the two men could cover a wide range of human
experience, but all of it quite normal ('in the broad highway of the
world'), despite its strangeness.

197–8 **native** natural, undisturbed. In a writer who values the churchyard
('The dead man's home') for being 'a fellow to [the] pasture field'
(ll. 170–1) – sharing its tranquillity and lack of adornment – it is clearly
significant that one particular grave should touch the primeval rock.

199–201 Another example of Wordsworth (or the Priest) imitating Shake-
speare's figurative language. Youth and age are seen as forces interact-
ing ('engendering' – the metaphor is a sexual one) to produce the old
man's peculiar vigour. Compare *Merchant of Venice*, III. ii. 67–8: 'It is
engendered in the eyes, / With gazing fed'.

202–4 The Ewbanks were generous people whose natural expansiveness
(the 'family heart' of l. 209) was restricted by the smallness of their
means.

208–14 The pastoral world of Wordsworth is isolated from the city, but not

They left to him the family heart, and land
With other burthens than the crop it bore!   2
Year after year the old man still preserved
A cheerful mind, and buffeted with bond,
Interest and mortgages, at last he sank,
And went into his grave before his time.
Poor Walter – whether it was care that spurred him   2
God only knows, but to the very last
He had the lightest foot in Ennerdale.
His pace was never that of an old man –
I almost see him tripping down the path
With his two grandsons after him. But you,   22
Unless our landlord be your host to-night,
Have far to travel, and in these rough paths
Even in the longest day of midsummer . . .

LEONARD

But these two orphans . . .

PRIEST

Orphans – such they were,
Yet not while Walter lived. For though their parents   22
Lay buried side by side as now they lie,
The old man was a father to the boys –
Two fathers in one father – and if tears
Shed when he talked of them where they were not,
And hauntings from the infirmity of love,   23
Are aught of what makes up a mother's heart,
This old man in the day of his old age
Was half a mother to them. If you weep, sir,
To hear a stranger talking about strangers,
Heaven bless you when you are among your kindred!   23
Aye, you may turn that way – it is a grave
Which will bear looking at.

protected from the realities of commercial life. Walter Ewbank and
Michael are freeholders, but the cost of their independence is that they
inherit land which has been heavily mortgaged.

221   That is, unless you plan to stay at our local inn.

228–33 Compare the emphasis in *Michael* on the old shepherd's having done
'female service' to Luke, and 'rocked / His cradle with a woman's gentle
hand' (ll. 162–8).

235   **kindred**   relatives.

LEONARD

These boys, I hope
They loved this good old man?

PRIEST

They did, and truly –
But that was what we almost overlooked,
They were such darlings of each other. For   240
Though from their cradles they had lived with Walter
The only kinsman near them in the house,
Yet he being old they had much love to spare,
And it all went into each other's hearts.
Leonard, the elder by just eighteen months,   245
Was two years taller – 'twas a joy to see,
To hear, to meet them! From their house the school
Was distant three short miles; and in the time
Of storm, and thaw, when every water-course
And unbridged stream (such as you may have noticed,   250
Crossing our roads at every hundred steps)
Was swoln into a noisy rivulet,
Would Leonard then, when elder boys perhaps
Remained at home, go staggering through the fords
Bearing his brother on his back. I've seen him   255
On windy days, in one of those stray brooks –
Aye, more than once I've seen him mid-leg deep,
Their two books lying both on a dry stone
Upon the hither side. And once I said,
As I remember, looking round these rocks   260
And hills on which we all of us were born,
That God who made the great book of the world
Would bless such piety.

LEONARD

It may be then . . .

---

263 **piety** virtue. The Priest's faith is of a fairly simple kind, and his
imagery suggests not only that God has made 'the great book of the
world' in which we are to 'read' His presence, but that He *keeps* a great
book, in which good deeds are totted up according to a system of reward
and punishment.

PRIEST

Never did worthier lads break English bread:
The finest Sunday that the autumn saw,
With all its mealy clusters of ripe nuts,
Could never keep these boys away from church,
Or tempt them to an hour of sabbath breach.
Leonard and James – I warrant, every corner
Among these rocks, and every hollow place
Where foot could come, to one or both of them
Was known as well as to the flowers that grow there.
Like roebucks they went bounding o'er the hills;
They played like two young ravens on the crags.
Then they could write, aye and speak too, as well
As many of their betters. And for Leonard –
The very night before he went away,
In my own house I put into his hand
A bible, and I'd wager twenty pounds
That if he is alive he has it yet.

LEONARD

It seems these brothers have not lived to be
A comfort to each other?

PRIEST

                    That they might
Live to that end, is what both old and young
In this our valley all of us have wished –
And what for my part I have often prayed.
But Leonard . . .

LEONARD

             Then James still is left among you?

268   **sabbath breach**   breaking of the Commandment to do no work on the
        Sabbath (Sunday).
273–4   Wordsworth's identification with Leonard and James at this point is
        seen in the recollection of *Tintern Abbey*, ll. 68–9: 'when like a roe / I
        bounded o'er the mountains'. In fact the image of the roebuck as
        embodying strength and swiftness goes back to The Song of Songs
        (Authorized Version): 'The voice of my beloved! behold he cometh
        leaping upon the mountains, skipping upon the hills. / My beloved is
        like a roe or a young hart . . . '

PRIEST

'Tis of the elder brother I am speaking –
They had an uncle (he was at that time
A thriving man and trafficked on the seas),
And but for this same uncle, to this hour   290
Leonard had never handled rope or shroud.
For the boy loved the life which we lead here;
And, though a very stripling, twelve years old,
His soul was knit to this his native soil.
But, as I said, old Walter was too weak   295
To strive with such a torrent. When he died,
The estate and house were sold, and all their sheep –
A pretty flock, and which, for aught I know,
Had clothed the Ewbanks for a thousand years.
Well – all was gone, and they were destitute;   300
And Leonard, chiefly for his brother's sake,
Resolved to try his fortune on the seas.
'Tis now twelve years since we had tidings from him.
If there was one among us who had heard
That Leonard Ewbank was come home again,   305
From the Great Gavel, down by Leeza's Banks,
And down the Enna, far as Egremont,
The day would be a very festival,
And those two bells of ours, which there you see
Hanging in the open air – but O good sir,   310
This is sad talk; they'll never sound for him,
Living or dead. When last we heard of him
He was in slavery among the Moors
Upon the Barbary Coast. 'Twas not a little
That would bring down his spirit, and no doubt   315
Before it ended in his death, the lad

---

294   **knit**   joined, closely united. Compare Walter Ewbank's grave touch-
      ing the native rock (ll. 197–8, above).
306–8 *The Great Gavel, so called I imagine from its resemblance to the gable-end of a*
       house, is one of the highest of the Cumberland mountains. It stands at the head of the
       several Vales of Ennerdale, Wastdale, and Borrowdale.
       The Leeza is a river which flows into the Lake of Ennerdale. On issuing from the
       Lake, it changes its name, and is called the End, Eyne, or Enna. It falls into the sea
       a little below Egremont. W.W.
314   **Barbary Coast**   the north coast of Africa.

Was sadly crossed. Poor Leonard, when we parted
He took me by the hand and said to me
If ever the day came when he was rich
He would return, and on his father's land
He would grow old among us.

LEONARD

If that day
Should come, 'twould needs be a glad day for him;
He would himself, no doubt, be happy then
As any that should meet him.

PRIEST

Happy, sir –

LEONARD

You said his kindred were all in their graves,
And that he had one brother . . .

PRIEST

That is but
A fellow tale of sorrow. From his youth
James, though not sickly, yet was delicate;
And Leonard being always by his side
Had done so many offices about him
That, though he was not of a timid nature,
Yet still the spirit of a mountain boy
In him was somewhat checked. And when his brother
Was gone to sea and he was left alone,
The little colour that he had was soon
Stolen from his cheek; he drooped and pined and pined . . .

LEONARD

But these are all the graves of full grown men . . .

---

317   **crossed**   caused to suffer. The word carries with it the implication of
'having a cross to bear'.
327   **fellow**   similar.
330   Had looked after him so much.
333–6   As he tells of James' loneliness, and makes use of the image of the
drooping flower, Wordsworth's thoughts go back to *The Ruined Cottage*;
see especially ll. 175, 392–6.

PRIEST

Aye, sir, that passed away. We took him to us –
He was the child of all the dale. He lived
Three months with one, and six months with another,   340
And wanted neither food, nor clothes, nor love;
And many, many happy days were his.
But, whether blithe or sad, 'tis my belief
His absent brother still was at his heart.
And when he lived beneath our roof, we found   345
(A practice till this time unknown to him)
That often, rising from his bed at night,
He in his sleep would walk about, and sleeping
He sought his brother Leonard. You are moved!
Forgive me, sir, before I spoke to you   350
I judged you most unkindly.

LEONARD

But this youth,
How did he die at last?

PRIEST

One sweet May morning
(It will be twelve years since, when spring returns)
He had gone forth among the new-dropped lambs
With two or three companions, whom it chanced   355
Some further business summoned to a house
Which stands at the dale-head. James, tired perhaps,
Or from some other cause, remained behind.
You see yon precipice? It almost looks
Like some vast building made up of many crags,   360
And in the midst is one particular rock
That rises like a column from the vale,
Whence by our shepherds it is called the Pillar.

345–9   Compare Margaret's compulsive seeking after Robert in *Ruined Cottage*, 348–51:

> Today
> I have been travelling far, and many days
> About the fields I wander, knowing this
> Only, that what I seek I cannot find.

353   James' death is carefully dated to the period just after the last news is heard of Leonard, 'in slavery among the Moors' (ll. 303, 312–13).

James pointed to its summit, over which
They all had purposed to return together,
And told them that he there would wait for them.
They parted, and his comrades passed that way
Some two hours after, but they did not find him
At the appointed place – a circumstance
Of which they took no heed – but one of them,
Going by chance, at night, into the house
Which at this time was James's home, there learned
That nobody had seen him all that day.
The morning came, and still he was unheard of;
The neighbours were alarmed, and to the brook
Some went, and some towards the lake. Ere noon
They found him at the foot of that same rock,
Dead, and with mangled limbs. The third day after,
I buried him poor lad, and there he lies.

LEONARD

And that then *is* his grave. Before his death
You said that he saw many happy years?

PRIEST

Aye, that he did –

LEONARD

And all went well with him?

PRIEST

If he had one, the lad had twenty homes.

LEONARD

And you believe then, that his mind was easy?

PRIEST

Yes, long before he died he found that time
Is a true friend to sorrow; and unless

364–73   A passage regarded by Coleridge in 1817 as 'metre to the eye only'
          (unrecognizable as verse even to the most delicate ear), and transcribed
          in a footnote to chapter XVIII of *Biographia Literaria* as continuous prose.
          Another view might be that the narrative is for the moment rather flat,
          and would be so equally in prose.

His thoughts were turned on Leonard's luckless fortune,
He talked about him with a chearful love.

LEONARD

He could not come to an unhallowed end?

PRIEST

Nay, God forbid! You recollect I mentioned   390
A habit which disquietude and grief
Had brought upon him; and we all conjectured
That as the day was warm he had lain down
Upon the grass, and waiting for his comrades
He there had fallen asleep – that in his sleep   395
He to the margin of the precipice
Had walked, and from the summit had fallen headlong.
And so no doubt he perished. At the time
We guess that in his hands he must have had
His shepherd's staff; for midway in the cliff   400
It had been caught, and there for many years
It hung – and mouldered there.

                The priest here ended.
The stranger would have thanked him, but he felt
Tears rushing in. Both left the spot in silence,
And Leonard, when they reached the churchyard gate,   405
As the priest lifted up the latch, turned round,
And looking at the grave he said, 'My brother'.
The vicar did not hear the words; and now,
Pointing towards the cottage, he entreated
That Leonard would partake his homely fare.   410
The other thanked him with a fervent voice,
But added that, the evening being calm,
He would pursue his journey. So they parted.

389   Attitudes towards suicide were changing – some parsons were, for instance, allowing suicides to be buried within the churchyard – but at the beginning of the nineteenth century it was still regarded as a sin. Compare *Ruined Cottage*, 339–54n.

399–402   See Introduction, pp. 13–14, for the story of Bowman and his staff, which was Wordsworth's starting-point in *The Brothers*, and also for the especially strong echoes of *The Ruined Cottage* found at this point in the poem.

It was not long ere Leonard reached a grove
That overhung the road. He there stopped short,
And sitting down beneath the trees, reviewed
All that the priest had said.

                        His early years
Were with him in his heart – his cherished hopes,
And thoughts which had been his an hour before,
All pressed on him with such a weight that now
This vale where he had been so happy seemed
A place in which he could not bear to live.
So he relinquished all his purposes.
He travelled on to Egremont; and thence
That night addressed a letter to the priest
Reminding him of what had passed between them,
And adding – with a hope to be forgiven –
That it was from the weakness of his heart
He had not dared to tell him who he was.
This done, he went on shipboard, and is now
A seaman, a grey-headed mariner.

414–17 Compare the moment just before the end of *The Ruined Cottage* in which the Poet 'leaning o'er the garden gate' *reviews* the sufferings of Margaret (ll. 497–8). The great difference of course is that Leonard has been told his own story.

Michael: A Pastoral Poem

If from the public way you turn your steps
Up the tumultuous brook of Greenhead Gill
You will suppose that with an upright path
Your feet must struggle, in such bold ascent
The pastoral mountains front you, face to face.   5
But courage! – for beside that boisterous brook
The mountains have all opened out themselves,
And made a hidden valley of their own.
No habitation there is seen; but such
As journey thither find themselves alone   10
With a few sheep, with rocks and stones, and kites
That overhead are sailing in the sky.
    It is in truth an utter solitude,
Nor should I have made mention of this dell
But for one object which you might pass by –   15
Might see and notice not. Beside the brook
There is a straggling heap of unhewn stones;

 1 Dorothy's *Journal* shows that *Michael* was written in October–December
   1800. In a note to the poem dictated at the end of his life, Wordsworth
   claimed that 'the character and circumstances of Luke' (and thus pre-
   sumably much of the central story) had been suggested by local
   memories of a family who once had owned Dove Cottage. See Introduc-
   tion, pp. 19–20, above, for letters to the Whig politician, Charles James
   Fox, and Thomas Poole, which discuss the special virtues of the Lake
   District 'statesman', or yeoman farmer – the class to which Michael
   belongs. And for Wordsworth's general assumption that country life
   allows 'the essential passions of the heart' to develop more freely (and
   to find expression in a plainer, more direct form of language), see the
   Preface to *Lyrical Ballads*, written just before *Michael*, in September 1800.
11–12 **kite**   a small bird of prey, common in Wordsworth's time.
13–17   Four very beautiful lines which Wordsworth at one stage intended to
   use when introducing the sheepfold are quoted Introduction, p. 18,
   above. Another draft which one can only feel sorry that he did not
   include in the final text, evokes the pleasure of coming on such 'vestiges
   of human hands' amid the wilds of Nature:
                                        For me
                When it has chanced that having wandered long
                Among the mountains I have waked at length

65

And to that place a story appertains,
Which, though it be ungarnished with events,
Is not unfit, I deem, for the fireside
Or for the summer shade. It was the first,
The earliest of those tales that spake to me
Of shepherds, dwellers in the vallies, men
Whom I already loved – not verily
For their own sakes, but for the fields and hills
Where was their occupation and abode.
And hence this tale, while I was yet a boy –
Careless of books, yet having felt the power
Of Nature – by the gentle agency
Of natural objects led me on to feel
For passions that were not my own, and think
(At random and imperfectly indeed)
On man, the heart of man, and human life.

> From dream of motion in some spot like this
> Shut out from man, some region – one of those
> That hold by an inalienable right
> An independent life, and seem the whole
> Of Nature, and of unrecorded time –
> If, looking round, I have perchance perceived
> Some vestiges of human hands, some stir
> Of human passion, they to me are sweet
> As light at day-break or the sudden sound
> Of music to a blind man's ear who sits
> Alone and silent in the summer shade.
> They are as a creation in my heart . . .
> (*Oxford Wordsworth*, II, 479–80)

19   **ungarnished**   not embellished, or made deliberately attractive.

19–21   Wordsworth invariably sounds priggish when contrasting his own uneventful poetry of the heart with the sensationalism found in his contemporaries (especially the Germans). Compare *Ruined Cottage*, 231–5, and *Hart-Leap Well*, 97–100, of January 1800:

> The moving accident is not my trade,
> To freeze the blood I have no ready arts;
> 'Tis my delight alone in summer shade
> To pipe a simple song to thinking hearts.

21–6   Book VIII of *The Prelude* is headed '*Love of Nature Leading to Love of Mankind*', and contains, among other material from 1800, a tale actually written for *Michael* (1805, VIII. 222–311).

33   Wordsworth is quoting almost verbatim from the first lines of the 'Prospectus', written at the beginning of the year for his great projected (and never in fact completed) philosophical work, *The Recluse*:

Therefore, although it be a history
Homely and rude, I will relate the same   35
For the delight of a few natural hearts –
And with yet fonder feeling for the sake
Of youthful poets who among these hills
Will be my second self when I am gone.
      Upon the forest-side in Grasmere vale   40
There dwelt a shepherd, Michael was his name,
An old man, stout of heart and strong of limb.
His bodily frame had been from youth to age
Of an unusual strength; his mind was keen,
Intense, and frugal, apt for all affairs;   45
And in his shepherd's calling he was prompt
And watchful more than ordinary men.
Hence he had learned the meaning of all winds,
Of blasts of every tone; and oftentimes
When others heeded not, he heard the south   50

       On man, on Nature, and on human life
       Thinking in solitude I oft perceive
       Fair chains of imagery before me rise . . .

An attempt in March to write the central section of *The Recluse* had produced some beautiful poetry in *Home at Grasmere*, but petered out as Wordsworth faced the difficulties of presenting the countryman's way of life as an ideal (see ll. 62–4n, below). Now in *Michael* he was trying again to do so, but within the form of a story.

37–9 Compare the end of *Tintern Abbey* (1798), where it is to be Dorothy who will be the poet's 'second self' when he is gone. Though only thirty when *Michael* was written, Wordsworth was preoccupied with different ways of achieving continuity, permanence, immortality.

40–2 To mark the opening of his tale Wordsworth in ll. 40–2 takes up a stance that is surely intended to bring Chaucer to the reader's mind. The 'forest-side' was the eastern side of the Vale, between Townend (and Dove Cottage) to the south, and Greenhead Ghyll beneath the slopes of Helvellyn to the north.

41–79 Quoted by Coleridge in *Biographia Literaria*, chapter XVII, as an example of poetry in which character and attributes are representative of a class (as Aristotle said they should be), not 'such as one gifted individual might possibly possess'.

44–7 Compare Wordsworth's statement the previous month in the Preface to *Lyrical Ballads* that poets are 'possessed of more than usual organic sensibility' (more innate, or natural, awareness). It often seems that Wordsworth identifies with Michael as he writes.

45 **apt for all affairs** suited to different kinds of work, adaptable.

50–2 Wordsworth is writing a poetry of numinous suggestion that cannot be translated or explained. He is as aware as the rest of us that the south

Make subterraneous music, like the noise
Of bagpipers on distant Highland hills.
The shepherd, at such warning, of his flock
Bethought him, and he to himself would say,
'The winds are now devising work for me!'   5
And truly at all times the storm that drives
The traveller to a shelter, summoned him
Up to the mountains: he had been alone
Amid the heart of many thousand mists
That came to him and left him on the heights.   6
So lived he till his eightieth year was passed;
And grossly that man errs who should suppose
That the green valleys, and the streams and rocks,
Were things indifferent to the shepherd's thoughts.
Fields, where with chearful spirits he had breathed   6

wind doesn't make an underground ('subterraneous') music. Compare
'The winds come to me from the fields of sleep' (*Intimations*, 28), and the
use of 'under' as a prefix in 1805 *Prelude*, III. 539–40, 'Hushed meanwhile
/ Was the under-soul.' See also ll. 58–60 below, where mists take over
from the wind, and again there is a delicate implication that Michael's
experience is more than ordinary.

62–4   Wordsworth's hectoring tones show unease, and the extent of his own
need to believe that Michael and others like him are responsive to the
beauty of their surroundings. *Home at Grasmere* had faltered to a stop six
months before precisely because he couldn't show in Grasmere
peasants a sensibility that would enable him to hold up their way of life
as an ideal. One unused draft of *Michael* presents the shepherd in an
imaginary conversation designed to bring out in him an underlying
love:

> No doubt if you in terms direct had asked
> Whether he loved the mountains, true it is
> That with blunt repetition of your words
> He might have stared at you, and said that they
> Were frightful to behold . . .
> [But] if it was his fortune to converse
> With any who could talk of common things
> In an unusual way, and give to them
> Unusual aspects, or by questions apt
> Wake sudden recognitions . . .
>   then, when he discoursed
> Of mountain sights, this untaught shepherd stood
> Before the man with whom he so conversed
> And looked at him as with a poet's eye.
>   (*Oxford Wordsworth*, II, 482)

The common air, the hills which he so oft
Had climbed with vigorous steps – which had impressed
So many incidents upon his mind
Of hardship, skill or courage, joy or fear;
Which like a book preserved the memory   70
Of the dumb animals whom he had saved,
Had fed or sheltered, linking to such acts,
So grateful in themselves, the certainty
Of honourable gains – these fields, these hills,
Which were his living being even more   75
Than his own blood (what could they less?), had laid
Strong hold on his affections, were to him
A pleasurable feeling of blind love,
The pleasure which there is in life itself.
     He had not passed his days in singleness: 80
He had a wife, a comely matron – old,
Though younger than himself full twenty years.
She was a woman of a stirring life,
Whose heart was in her house. Two wheels she had
Of antique form – this, large for spinning wool,   85
That, small for flax – and if one wheel had rest
It was because the other was at work.

70–4   The fields and hills are a record of countless minor incidents that
would be forgotten were it not that every time Michael sees or visits a
particular spot it impresses on him memories of what has happened
there in the past. To the pleasant ('grateful') thoughts of having saved,
or fed, or sheltered, his animals, is linked the fact that doing so was
profitable. The image of the fields and hills as a book is recalled in
Wordsworth's letter to Fox, when he says that the 'land serves as a kind
of permanent rallying-point for . . . domestic feelings – as a tablet upon
which they are written, which makes them objects of memory in a
thousand instances when they would otherwise be forgotten' (*EY*, 315).

74–6   Wordsworth's primary meaning is that Michael's life consisted of, or
depended upon, the fields and hills even more than it did on the blood
in his veins. 'Blood' can, however, mean 'blood relation', and there is
thus a possible secondary reading – appropriate especially when one
knows the tragic outcome of the story – that Michael values the land
still more than he values his son.

81   **comely** good looking. **matron** used of women of middle age and
upwards, to imply dignity and perhaps motherliness.

84–7   Some of Michael's wool would be sold as whole fleeces, but it was an
advantage to spin as much as possible. In her *Journal* for 24 November
1801, Dorothy records that the Ashburner family across the road from
Dove Cottage have paid off £100 of their taxes by getting up to spin at

counting

The pair had but one inmate in their house,
An only child, who had been born to them
When Michael telling o'er his years began   9
To deem that he was old – in shepherd's phrase,
With one foot in the grave. This only son,
With two brave sheep dogs tried in many a storm
(The one of an inestimable worth),
Made all their household. I may truly say   9
That they were as a proverb in the vale
For endless industry. When day was gone,
And from their occupations out of doors
The son and father were come home, even then
Their labour did not cease, unless when all   I
Turned to their cleanly supper-board, and there
Each with a mess of pottage and skimmed milk,
Sate round their basket piled with oaten cakes,
And their plain home-made cheese. Yet when their meal
Was ended, Luke (for so the son was named)   I
And his old father both betook themselves
To such convenient work as might employ
Their hands by the fireside – perhaps to card
Wool for the housewife's spindle, or repair
Some injury done to sickle, flail, or scythe,   I
Or other implement of house or field.
        Down from the ceiling by the chimney's edge
(Which in our ancient uncouth country style

deity.

5 o'clock every morning. Flax was grown locally for the weaving of linen, and Isabel, like Margaret in her last years (*Ruined Cottage*, 459–62), would have been paid according to the amount of spinning she was able to do. I am grateful to John West, Curator of Hawkshead School, for information on these matters.

88   **one inmate in their house**   one person living with them.

102 **mess of pottage**   usually a bowl of soup, but here porridge. Wordsworth probably thought of the phrase as biblical (see, for example, Genesis, 25. 29–34).

108–11   One thinks of Michael simply as a sheep farmer, but his implements show that in the lower fields he grew not only hay (cut with the scythe), but also corn (probably oats), cut with the scythe, and threshed with the flail. The men's carding of wool recalls *Brothers*, 20–3, and their mending of implements implies an exactly opposite frame of mind to Robert's in *The Ruined Cottage* as he idly seeks 'through every nook / Of house or garden any casual task / Of use or ornament' (ll. 166–8).

Did with a huge projection overbrow
Large space beneath) as duly as the light   115
Of day grew dim, the housewife hung a lamp,
An aged utensil which had performed
Service beyond all others of its kind.
Early at evening did it burn, and late,
Surviving comrade of uncounted hours   120
Which going by from year to year had found
And left the couple neither gay perhaps
Nor chearful, yet with objects and with hopes
Living a life of eager industry.
And now, when Luke was in his eighteenth year,   125
There by the light of this old lamp they sate,
Father and son, while late into the night
The housewife plied her own peculiar work,
Making the cottage through the silent hours
Murmur as with the sound of summer flies.   130
Not with a waste of words, but for the sake
Of pleasure which I know that I shall give
To many living now, I of this lamp
Speak thus minutely; for there are no few
Whose memories will bear witness to my tale.   135
The light was famous in its neighbourhood,
And was a public symbol of the life
The thrifty pair had lived. For, as it chanced,
Their cottage on a plot of rising ground
Stood single, with large prospect north and south,   140
High into Easedale, up to Dunmal-Raise,
And westward to the village near the Lake.
And from this constant light so regular

114   **overbrow** overshadow, overhang like a brow.
119–24   The hours (l. 120) are both 'countless' and *not counted*, in that the
          couple do not reckon up their working time. *Ruined Cottage*, 121–30 con-
          firms that for Wordsworth work done in addition to one's main job was
          a sign of industry and happiness. The possibility of having the lamp
          alight for mere pleasure was presumably ruled out by expense.
128   **peculiar** particular.
130   For a passage describing Michael's conversation that Wordsworth in
          April 1801 thought of inserting before l. 131 (together with some
          changes to ll. 131–5), see *EY*, 324.
143–6   In describing Michael and Isabel's 'life of eager industry', and dwell-
          ing on the lamp that sheds its influence wide over the vale, Wordsworth
          was privately aware of a parallel with himself and Dorothy. In the Pros-

[handwritten: real-life / naming]

And so far-seen, the house itself by all
Who dwelt within the limits of the vale,
Both old and young, was named The Evening Star.
     Thus living on through such a length of years
The shepherd, if he loved himself, must needs
Have loved his help-mate; but to Michael's heart
This son of his old age was yet more dear –
Effect which might perhaps have been produced
By that instinctive tenderness, the same
Blind spirit which is in the blood of all,
Or that a child more than all other gifts,
Brings hope with it, and forward-looking thoughts,
And stirrings of inquietude, when they
By tendency of Nature needs must fail.
From such, and other causes, to the thoughts
Of the old man his only son was now
The dearest object that he knew on earth.
Exceeding was the love he bare to him,
His heart and his heart's joy! For oftentimes
Old Michael, while he was a babe in arms,
Had done him female service, not alone
For dalliance and delight, as is the use
Of fathers, but with patient mind enforced
To acts of tenderness; and he had rocked

pectus to *The Recluse*, written at the beginning of the year, he had prayed
that his own work should 'live, and be / Even as a light hung up in
heaven to cheer / The world in times to come'. There was apparently a
house on high ground to the north of Dove Cottage that had earned the
name of The Evening Star.

150 **This son of his old age**   see ll. 342–3n, below.

156–7 It is important to notice that Wordsworth valued the 'stirrings of
inquietude' (feelings of restlessness, of being forced out of one's settled
ways) as highly as the 'hope and forward-looking thoughts'. He dreaded
the effects of age ('the tendency of Nature' that causes our faculties to
fail) especially because he associated 'stirrings of inquietude' with the
creative impulse – the 'Poetic spirit of our human life' which for most
people is 'abated and suppressed' by the passing of time (1799 *Prelude*,
II, 306–8).

161–2 The archaic use of 'exceeding' and 'bare' (for 'bore'), together with
the inverted word order, show that in describing Michael's relationship
with Luke, Wordsworth is consciously evoking the Bible; see ll. 342–3n,
below.

164 **done him female service**   tended to him as if he (Michael) were a
woman.

His cradle with a woman's gentle hand.
    And in a later time, ere yet the boy
Had put on boy's attire, did Michael love   170
(Albeit of a stern unbending mind)
To have the young one in his sight when he
Had work by his own door, or when he sate
With sheep before him on his shepherd's stool
Beneath that large old oak, which near their door   175
Stood, and from its enormous breadth of shade
Chosen for the shearer's covert from the sun,
Thence in our rustic dialect was called
The Clipping Tree – a name which yet it bears.
There, while they two were sitting in the shade   180
With others round them, earnest all and blithe,
Would Michael exercise his heart with looks
Of fond correction and reproof, bestowed
Upon the child if he disturbed the sheep
By catching at their legs, or with his shouts   185
Scared them while they lay still beneath the shears.
And when by Heaven's good grace the boy grew up
A healthy lad, and carried in his cheek
Two steady roses that were five years old,
Then Michael from a winter coppice cut   190
With his own hand a sapling, which he hooped
With iron, making it throughout in all
Due requisites a perfect shepherd's staff,
And gave it to the boy; wherewith equipped,
He as a watchman oftentimes was placed   195
At gate or gap, to stem or turn the flock;
And, to his office prematurely called,
There stood the urchin, as you will divine,
Something between a hindrance and a help –

169–70 Boys wore skirts until they were 'breeched' (put into breeches) at the
        age of seven or eight. Compare Coleridge's reference to his sister in
        Frost at Midnight (1798), 43, 'My playmate when we both were clothed
        alike'.
177   **covert** shade, shelter.
179   *Clipping is the word used in the North of England for shearing.* W.W.
188–9   A case of poetic diction which, given the preface to *Lyrical Ballads*, one
        might have expected Wordsworth to avoid. Luke was five.
190   **coppice** copse – a small wood.
196   **stem** stop. 197 **office** task, job. 198 **divine** guess.

And for this cause not always, I believe,   2C
Receiving from his father hire of praise,
Though nought was left undone which staff, or voice,
Or looks, or threatening gestures, could perform.
But soon as Luke, full ten years old, could stand
Against the mountain blasts, and to the heights,   20
Not fearing toil, nor length of weary ways,
He with his father daily went, and they
Were as companions – why should I relate
That objects which the shepherd loved before
Were dearer now? – that from the boy there came   21
Feelings and emanations, things which were
Light to the sun and music to the wind,
And that the old man's heart seemed born again?
Thus in his father's sight the boy grew up
And now when he had reached his eighteenth year,   21
He was his comfort and his daily hope.

     While this good household thus were living on
From day to day, to Michael's ear there came
Distressful tidings. Long before the time   _event_
Of which I speak, the shepherd had been bound   22
In surety for his brother's son, a man
Of an industrious life and ample means,
But unforeseen misfortunes suddenly
Had pressed upon him, and old Michael now
Was summoned to discharge the forfeiture –   22
A grievous penalty, but little less
Than half his substance. This unlooked-for claim,
At the first hearing, for a moment took
More hope out of his life than he supposed
That any old man ever could have lost.   23
As soon as he had gathered so much strength

201   **hire** reward.

210–12 On an ordinary reading, Luke's 'emanations' are expressions of joy
     that heighten his father's pleasure in the sun and wind. But this is to
     ignore Wordsworth's tender and uncharacteristic use of hyperbole to
     evoke the greatness of Michael's love. Luke becomes the source of life,
     giving light to the life-giving sun, and providing the wind with its music.

220–1 Michael has guaranteed a loan for his nephew, offering his land as
     security.

225 **discharge the forfeiture** pay the sum he had guaranteed on the loan.

226–7 **but little . . . substance** only a little less than half his capital.

That he could look his trouble in the face,
It seemed that his sole refuge was to sell
A portion of his patrimonial fields.
Such was his first resolve; he thought again,   235
And his heart failed him. 'Isabel', said he,
Two evenings after he had heard the news,
'I have been toiling more than seventy years,
And in the open sunshine of God's love
Have we all lived, yet if these fields of ours   240
Should pass into a stranger's hand, I think
That I could not lie quiet in my grave.
Our lot is a hard lot; the sun itself
Has scarcely been more diligent than I,
And I have lived to be a fool at last   245
To my own family. An evil man
That was, and made an evil choice, if he
Were false to us; and if he were not false,
There are ten thousand to whom loss like this
Had been no sorrow. I forgive him – but   250
'Twere better to be dumb than to talk thus.
When I began, my purpose was to speak
Of remedies, and of a chearful hope.
Our Luke shall leave us, Isabel; the land
Shall not go from us, and it shall be free –   255
He shall possess it, free as is the wind
That passes over it. We have, thou knowest,
Another kinsman; he will be our friend
In this distress. He is a prosperous man,
Thriving in trade, and Luke to him shall go   260
And with his kinsman's help and his own thrift
He quickly will repair this loss, and then
May come again to us. If here he stay,
What can be gained?'
                    At this the old man paused
And Isabel sat silent, for her mind   265
Was busy looking back into past times.

---

234   **patrimonial fields**   land that he had inherited from his fathers.
243   **lot**   fate, way of life.
245–6   It is difficult to find an exact parallel to Wordsworth's use of 'fool',
      but Michael clearly feels both that he has played the fool with the family
      fortunes, and that he has been made a fool of.

'There's Richard Bateman', thought she to herself,
'He was a parish-boy – at the church door
They made a gathering for him, shillings, pence,
And halfpennies, wherewith the neighbours bought
A basket, which they filled with pedlar's wares,
And with this basket on his arm the lad
Went up to London, found a master there,
Who out of many chose the trusty boy
To go and overlook his merchandise
Beyond the seas, where he grew wondrous rich
And left estates and monies to the poor,
And at his birthplace built a chapel, floored
With marble which he sent from foreign lands.'
These thoughts, and many others of like sort,
Passed quickly through the mind of Isabel,
And her face brightened. The old man was glad,
And thus resumed: 'Well, Isabel, this scheme
These two days has been meat and drink to me:
Far more than we have lost is left us yet.
We have enough – I wish indeed that I
Were younger, but this hope is a good hope.
Make ready Luke's best garments; of the best
Buy for him more, and let us send him forth
Tomorrow, or the next day, or tonight –
If he could go, the boy should go tonight.'
      Here Michael ceased, and to the fields went forth
With a light heart. The housewife for five days
Was restless morn and night, and all day long
Wrought on with her best fingers to prepare
Things needful for the journey of her son.
But Isabel was glad when Sunday came
To stop her in her work; for when she lay
By Michael's side, she for the last two nights
Heard him, how he was troubled in his sleep;
And when they rose at morning she could see

267   *The story alluded to here is well known in the country* [*the district*]. *The chapel is
      called Ings Chapel, and is on the right hand side of the road leading from Kendal to
      Ambleside.* W.W.
      Richard Bateman's marble floor may still be seen, but the church is to
      the left of the modern road.
295   **Wrought on with her best fingers**   worked as quickly as she could.
      Compare the phrase, 'to put one's best foot forward'.

That all his hopes were gone. That day at noon
She said to Luke, while they two by themselves
Were sitting at the door: 'Thou must not go,
We have no other child but thee to lose, 305
None to remember – do not go away,
For if thou leave thy father he will die.'
The lad made answer with a jocund voice,
And Isabel, when she had told her fears,
Recovered heart. That evening her best fare 310
Did she bring forth, and all together sate
Like happy people round a Christmas fire.
　　　Next morning Isabel resumed her work,
And all the ensuing week the house appeared
As cheerful as a grove in spring. At length 315
The expected letter from their kinsman came,
With kind assurances that he would do
His utmost for the welfare of the boy –
To which requests were added that forthwith
He might be sent to him. Ten times or more 320
The letter was read over; Isabel
Went forth to shew it to the neighbours round;
Nor was there at that time on English land
A prouder heart than Luke's. When Isabel
Had to her house returned the old man said, 325
'He shall depart to-morrow.' To this word
The housewife answered, talking much of things
Which, if at such short notice he should go,
Would surely be forgotten – but at length
She gave consent, and Michael was at ease. 330
　　　Near the tumultuous brook of Greenhead Gill
In that deep valley, Michael had designed
To build a sheepfold, and before he heard
The tidings of his melancholy loss
For this same purpose he had gathered up 335
A heap of stones, which close to the brook-side

308　**jocund**　joyful.
332–3　*It may be proper to inform some readers that a sheepfold in these mountains is an unroofed building of stone walls, with different divisions. It is generally placed by the side of a brook, for the convenience of washing the sheep; but it is also useful as a shelter for them, and as a place to drive them into, to enable the shepherds conveniently to single out one or more for any particular purpose. W.W.*

Summing in (being understood) in land or son.

Lay thrown together, ready for the work.
With Luke that evening thitherward he walked,
And soon as they had reached the place he stopped,
And thus the old man spake to him: 'My son,
To-morrow thou wilt leave me. With full heart
I look upon thee, for thou art the same
That wert a promise to me ere thy birth,
And all thy life hast been my daily joy.
I will relate to thee some little part
Of our two histories; 'twill do thee good
When thou art from me, even if I should speak
Of things thou canst not know of. After thou
First camest into the world, as it befalls
To newborn infants, thou didst sleep away
Two days, and blessings from thy father's tongue
Then fell upon thee. Day by day passed on,
And still I loved thee with increasing love.
Never to living ear came sweeter sounds
Than when I heard thee by our own fireside
First uttering without words a natural tune –
When thou, a feeding babe, didst in thy joy
Sing at thy mother's breast. Month followed month,
And in the open fields my life was passed,
And in the mountains, else I think that thou
Hadst been brought up upon thy father's knees.
But we were playmates, Luke; among these hills,
As well thou knowest, in us the old and young
Have played together – nor with me didst thou
Lack any pleasure which a boy can know.'
        Luke had a manly heart; but at these words
He sobbed aloud. The old man grasped his hand,
And said, 'Nay do not take it so – I see

property

338   **thitherward**   in that direction, to that place.
342–3   Michael's strange, impressive statement (meaning presumably that
Isabel's pregnancy meant that there was suddenly a prospect of hand-
ing on the land within the family) brings in associations of Isaac,
Samson, and John the Baptist, all of them children of their fathers' old
age, and promised (by angels) before their birth.
348–52   Described by Wordsworth to Lamb in 1801 as one of the best
passages he ever wrote, 'combining in an extraordinary degree [the]
union of imagination and tenderness' (*Letters of Charles and Mary Anne
Lamb*, ed. Edwin W.J. Marrs [3 vols., Ithaca N.Y., 1975–8] I, 272–3).

That these are things of which I need not speak.
Even to the utmost I have been to thee   370
A kind and a good father; and herein
I but repay a gift which I myself
Received at others' hands, for though now old
Beyond the common life of man I still
Remember them who loved me in my youth.   375
Both of them sleep together – here they lived
As all their forefathers had done; and when
At length their time was come, they were not loth
To give their bodies to the family mold.
I wished that thou should'st live the life they lived;   380
But 'tis a long time to look back, my son,
And see so little gain from sixty years.
These fields were burthened when they came to me;
Till I was forty years of age, not more
Than half of my inheritance was mine.   385
I toiled and toiled; God blessed me in my work,
And till these three weeks past the land was free –
It looks as if it never could endure
Another master. Heaven forgive me, Luke,
If I judge ill for thee, but it seems good   390
That thou should'st go.'
                 At this the old man paused,
Then pointing to the stones near which they stood,
Thus after a short silence he resumed:
'This was a work for us, and now, my son,
It is a work for me. But, lay one stone –   395
Here, lay it for me, Luke, with thine own hands –
I for the purpose brought thee to this place.
Nay, boy, be of good hope, we both may live
To see a better day. At eighty-four
I still am strong and stout; do thou thy part,   400
I will do mine. I will begin again
With many tasks that were resigned to thee;
Up to the heights, and in among the storms,

374   'The days of our age are threescore years and ten' (Psalm 95).
379   **mold**   the earth from which man was formed in Genesis, and to which
        he returns in the grave.
383–5   Walter Ewbank too inherits the burden of a mortgage with his land
        (*Brothers*, 212–15), but is never able to pay it off.

Will I without thee go again, and do
All works which I was wont to do alone
Before I knew thy face. Heaven bless thee,
Thy heart these two weeks has been beating fast
With many hopes. It should be so – yes, yes,
I knew that thou could'st never have a wish
To leave me, Luke – thou hast been bound to me
Only by links of love. When thou art gone
What will be left to us? – but I forget
My purposes. Lay now the corner-stone
As I requested, and hereafter, Luke,
When thou art gone away, should evil men
Be thy companions, let this sheepfold be
Thy anchor and thy shield. Amid all fear,
And all temptation, let it be to thee
An emblem of the life thy fathers lived,
Who, being innocent, did for that cause
Bestir them in good deeds. Now, fare thee well.
When thou return'st, thou in this place wilt see
A work which is not here. A covenant
'Twill be between us – but whatever fate
Befall thee, I shall love thee to the last,
And bear thy memory with me to the grave.'
        The shepherd ended here, and Luke stooped down
And as his father had requested, laid
The first stone of the sheepfold. At the sight
The old man's grief broke from him; to his heart
He pressed his son, he kissed him and wept –
And to the house together they returned.
Next morning, as had been resolved, the boy
Began his journey; and when he had reached
The public way he put on a bold face,

413–24   Though Wordsworth has no specific parallel in mind, he is drawing
        on biblical associations to create our sense that a ritual is being enacted.
        The words 'corner-stone' and 'covenant' are especially resonant in
        Christian tradition, the Old Testament depending on a covenant
        (mutual agreement) between God and the Children of Israel in Exodus,
        and the New being built on the corner-stone of Christ himself: 'the
        stone which the builders rejected'. For good measure, Peter is the rock
        on which the Church is founded.
431   **kissed**   though it sounds unnatural to modern ears, Wordsworth
        stressed the 'ed' – 'he kissèd him and wept'.

And all the neighbours as he passed their doors
Came forth with wishes and with farewell prayers
That followed him till he was out of sight.
  A good report did from their kinsman come
Of Luke and his well-doing; and the boy   440
Wrote loving letters, full of wondrous news,
Which, as the housewife phrased it, were throughout
The prettiest letters that were ever seen.
Both parents read them with rejoicing hearts.
So many months passed on, and once again   445
The shepherd went about his daily work
With confident and cheerful thoughts; and now
Sometimes when he could find a leisure hour
He to that valley took his way, and there
Wrought at the sheepfold. Meantime Luke began   450
To slacken in his duty, and at length
He in the dissolute city gave himself
To evil courses; ignominy and shame
Fell on him, so that he was driven at last
To seek a hiding-place beyond the seas.   455
  There is a comfort in the strength of love,
'Twill make a thing endurable which else
Would break the heart – old Michael found it so.
I have conversed with more than one who well
Remember the old man, and what he was   460
Years after he had heard this heavy news.
His bodily frame had been from youth to age
Of an unusual strength. Among the rocks
He went, and still looked up upon the sun,
And listened to the wind, and, as before,   465

444   It is interesting that Margaret in *The Ruined Cottage*, Leonard in *The
      Brothers*, and the whole of Michael's family are able to read. As Coleridge
      points out in *Biographia Literaria*, chapter XVII, despite the Preface to
      Lyrical Ballads Wordsworth's characters 'are by no means taken "from
      low or rustic life" in the common acceptation of those words'. Their
      social position is always such as to give them a certain independence.
452–4 Wordsworth was not as biassed against the city as this kind of state-
      ment makes him sound. In fact for some reason almost all his most
      unbalanced comments (including the description of Londoners as
      'slaves unrespited of low pursuits', *1805*, VII, 701) were written at the
      time of *Michael*. Perhaps he was feeling defensive about having with-
      drawn to live permanently in the country.

Performed all kinds of labour for his sheep
And for the land, his small inheritance.
And to that hollow dell from time to time
Did he repair, to build the fold of which
His flock had need. 'Tis not forgotten yet
The pity which was then in every heart
For the old man; and 'tis believed by all
That many and many a day he thither went,
And never lifted up a single stone.

 There by the sheepfold sometimes was he seen
Sitting alone, with that his faithful dog –
Then old – beside him, lying at his feet.
The length of full seven years from time to time
He at the building of this sheepfold wrought,
And left the work unfinished when he died.
Three years, or little more, did Isabel
Survive her husband; at her death the estate
Was sold, and went into a stranger's hand.
The cottage which was named The Evening Star
Is gone; the ploughshare has been through the ground
On which it stood. Great changes have been wrought
In all the neighbourhood; yet the oak is left
That grew beside their door, and the remains
Of the unfinished sheepfold may be seen
Beside the boisterous brook of Greenhead Gill.

487–8 Like the elms that stand beside Margaret's ruined cottage, the oak
  survives as the representative of an abiding and dispassionate natural
  order. Man comes, and man goes; the trees remain.